PRAISE FOR JOHN WIELAND

"I devoured this book and will reflect back upon it for the rest of my life. The stories John Wieland shares about his family, business, leadership, faith, community, kindness and humility will touch your very soul. At times raw and at times humorous, *Uncommon Threads* imparts life lessons that will motivate you to be a better human being."

— LIZ RICHARDS, CEO, MATERIAL HANDLING
EQUIPMENT DISTRIBUTORS ASSOCIATION

"*Uncommon Threads* weaves together John Wieland's experiences and the lessons he's learned as a tremendously successful businessman, loving family man and believer. It's an entertaining, thought-provoking, inspirational guide to living life honestly. Readers are lucky to be taken along on Wieland's ride."

— CHUCK WEAVER, RETIRED ILLINOIS STATE
SENATOR, ENTREPRENEUR AND PHILANTHROPIST

"*Uncommon Threads* is inspirational, honest and transparent. Packed with wise and practical advice as well as wonderful illustrations, this is an altogether refreshing book."

— MONICA SCHEUER RN, MS, RD, LD, EXECUTIVE DIRECTOR OF MIDWEST FOOD BANK

UNCOMMON THREADS

Weaving a Life Through Family, Business and Faith

JOHN WIELAND

Illustrated by Jim Boerckel

ISBN: 978-1-951407-81-0 hardcover

ISBN: 978-1-951407-70-4 paperback

ISBN: 978-1-951407-69-8 ebook

To my mom and dad. I miss you!
To Julie for being my life partner and for the grace that you show
To my children, Jessica, Jennifer, Jamie and Josiah, for the
privilege of being called your dad
To The Carpenter who died that the grave could not hold.

DISCLAIMER

This work is nonfiction and, as such, reflects the author's memory of the experiences. Many of the names and identifying characteristics of the individuals featured in this book have been changed to protect their privacy, and certain individuals are composites. Dialogue and events have been recreated; in some cases, conversations were edited to convey their substance rather than written exactly as they occurred.

CONTENTS

Introduction   xi

PART I
FAMILY

1. Call Me Johnny Awful   3
2. Four Adoptions and One Abortion   20
3. Prepare the Child for the Road, Not the Road   33
   for Your Child
4. Who Is Your Neighbor?   48
5. I've Got Your Back   57
6. Differences Are What Make the World Go   61
   Round
7. A Christian and a Muslim Meet at the   69
   Airport
8. Jerseyville, Where a Lot of White People Live   73

PART II
BUSINESS

9. A Safe Place   83
10. My Very Own Arch Nemesis   88
11. Welcome to MH Equipment   91
12. Leading Leaders   107
13. Values and Culture Are the Secret Sauce   125
14. Interesting People   161
15. Count the Cost?   169
16. Know All the Facts   174
17. Money   179
18. Never Die an Idiot   195
19. You Can Only Give What You Got   199

PART III
FAITH

20. A Mature Christian Versus a Drunk Teenager   215
21. In the Hands of the Miracle Man   220

22. Lasting Contentment   225
23. So You Want to Take Jesus to the Office   233
24. Lessons Learned from a Bone Marrow   243
    Transplant

    The Most Baffling of All   264

    Notes   269
    Acknowledgments   271
    About the Author   273

INTRODUCTION

Start with the end in mind.

When I told friends that I was writing a book, the encouragement most offered to me was: "Start with the end in mind." This proved to be harder than I expected.

I love Jesus a lot, but I didn't want this to be a "Christian Book." I have stories from my personal and family life, but I didn't want this to be my memoir. When I bought MH Equipment, it was virtually bankrupt. It now has 30 branches and over $300 million in revenue. While I know that our principles, values and culture drove our growth and success, I didn't want this to be simply a business book.

So why was the advice from my friends so tricky?

The reason is that *everything is connected*.

Family affects who you are. Business affects who you are. And your faith (or worldview) affects who you are. And each area impacts the others.

If I were going to diagram it, this is what it would look like:

It's the Triangle of Life.

All three are interconnected.

We all know that early family experiences go a long way toward influencing (but not necessarily deciding) who we become. Family experience can launch us successfully into adulthood or feel like a noose around the neck. Even though everyone has experiences on both ends of the scale, there is typically a heavy leaning one way or the other.

Business affects who we become, and it can be a dangerous monster if it becomes addictive, leading to a ruined family life and ruined faith. As an executive I know once said to me, "I am a Christian, but I will not let that get in the way of taking care of business." But business can also become a platform to positively impact those around you.

Faith is the foundation of how someone sees the world and how things ought to be. There are countless examples of how people of faith have positively changed the world because they lived out their faith. Unfortunately, there have also been atrocities committed because of *how* people interpreted and lived out their faith.

An infamous example of how these three affect each other is Kenneth Lay, the founder, CEO and Chairman of Enron. Lay was born in the small town of Tyrone, Missouri, the son of Ruth (born Rees) and Omer Lay. Lay's father was a Baptist preacher, and Lay grew up in poverty. A small town, a pastor for a dad. I'm sure Ken knew right from wrong. He surely knew that it is wrong to take advantage of people, and yet he was heavily involved in the Enron scandal.

When Enron went bankrupt in 2001, it was the biggest bankruptcy in US history. In total, 20,000 employees lost their jobs and in many cases their life savings. Investors also lost billions of dollars. On July 7, 2004, Lay was indicted by a grand jury in Houston, Texas for his role in the company's failure. He was charged with 11 counts of securities fraud, wire fraud and making misleading statements. In January of 2006, he was found guilty of 10 counts of securities fraud.

Lay died in July 2006 while vacationing in his house near Aspen, Colorado, a full three months before his scheduled sentencing. A preliminary autopsy reported that he died of a myocardial infarction (a heart attack) caused by coronary artery disease.

The Lays gave millions and millions away to charities. He went to church. His friends would say he was a true believer. So how does one go from the church pew to destroying the financial lives of thousands?

One word: Compartmentalization.

Compartmentalizing your world view and business creates incredible dysfunction and tremendous stress. This internal conflict simply does not go away. I know personally that when there is not harmony between these three, it negatively impacts the mind, body and spirit. I can't help but think that the stress of living two separate lives played a huge part in Kenneth Lay's death.

My commitment to not compartmentalizing is why this book contains three sections. It explores how family, business and faith ultimately fit together like a jigsaw puzzle.

Part One looks at some of my favorite personal and family experiences that laid the foundation I've carried throughout life.

Part Two examines some of the beliefs I hold in order to run a successful business that I believe are just as relevant whether you are leading a company or working for it. There are also short anecdotes about what I learned in business that affected my family and faith.

Part Three is about the beauty, tension and failures I've experienced as I have tried to live out my faith—and how that has played an important part in business. Please understand that when the imperfect (me) talks about the Perfect (God), by definition there is hypocrisy. I want to be clear at the outset: I have not "arrived" spiritually. We are all a work in process.

My hope is that you will laugh and cry, enjoy and study the incredible illustrations that my missionary friend Jim Boerkel has provided and hopefully be inspired. I also hope that you'll see how this book affirms that these three vital elements—family, business and faith—interact with that thing we call *life*.

Blessings.

PART I

FAMILY

CHAPTER 1

CALL ME JOHNNY AWFUL

Friends that know me and then meet my parents come away with a very strong opinion…

…You got lucky, John.

But I need to share a secret about growing up in the Wieland home. A lot of people think our house was peaceful, filled with grace and love, and that all people were welcomed to our home regardless of their station in life. Well, my three siblings and I lived there and we have to admit something: it was all true.

My dad grew up on a farm, went to school and became a doctor. Mom was raised by a Presbyterian minister and met Dad at nursing school. They were good, moral, kind and gracious people…they claim that they were both virgins on their wedding day—and I believe them!

My father was a medical doctor in the army, and he and Mom were stationed in Fort Sill, Oklahoma when I arrived on this earth on August 4, 1958. If there's one thing about my dad that says more about him than any other, it's this:

he didn't want a military funeral, not because he didn't love our country or respect the military he served, but because he felt he wasn't worthy of the honor. His rationale was that young men and women have stood in harm's way to protect our freedoms, and as someone not directly involved in battle, he didn't deserve the same honor in death. That's the kind of guy my dad was, and I understood and respected his position.

Dad's connections as a doctor came in handy for me early on, when I wasn't breathing well as a baby and the doctor who delivered me wanted to be extra attentive to one of his peers. So he did more tests than normal and discovered I had a collapsed lung. Thankfully, the doctor and his staff took care of it, but without getting ahead of the condition, who knows?

When most people think of their home, they think of two homes—the one where they currently live and the one where they were raised. "Home," to me, is my childhood home in Jerseyville, Illinois, where Mom and Dad lived their entire lives. There is a sense of stability when I can go back to my childhood home. My heart goes out to the many people who did not have a positive upbringing and for whom going back to a certain house is the farthest thing from stability.

Mom and Dad did a lovely job when it came to naming the girls in the family—my sisters' names, Felicia and Melanie, just roll off the tongue. But when they had boys, somehow all they could come up with was John and Dick. To make up for that lack of creativity, Dad gave us boys nicknames. He called Dick "Magic." Pretty cool, right? You have to admit that that's a great nickname to affirm that you are special to your parents.

Dad gave me a nickname too and it was awful. And I don't mean that it was an awful nickname. I mean that the nickname was simply "Awful." Yep, Dick was referred to as "Magic!" John, on the other hand, was Johnny Awful. Now before you start to think that my dad was a terrible father, or that I must have really been an awful kid to deserve such a name, please know that he was usually laughing at some irreverent behavior of mine when he called me "Awful." So if a father can call a son "awful" and also demonstrate tremendous affection, Dad somehow pulled it off. Words are important but how words are communicated is even more important.

All families have dysfunction and we were no different, but there was always a consistency at our house that was really an incredible blessing.

Everyone, and I mean everyone, seemed to like Mom and Dad.

Put it this way: I thought I was really popular in high school. We had a swimming pool so there were always parties and people over at the house. I was one cool guy. Then when I was at college, I'd be talking to Mom or Dad and they'd say, "Oh, so-and-so stopped by to say hi. So-and-so had lunch with us. So and so had dinner with us." We're not talking once in a while; I'd hear this sort of thing dozens of times a year. And whenever it happened, I'd think, "Well, that's odd, because those guys didn't stay in touch with me." Then it finally occurred to me: I wasn't the popular one. Mom and Dad were the popular people and I was just window dressing. Man, did that stink.

I'd love to tell you that I came to be just as well-liked as my parents but the truth is that years later, when Mom and Dad were in Louisville, I encouraged them to have dinner with one of the owners of MH Equipment, Bill and his wife, Susan. Big mistake. Bill had always thought I was a decent guy and had told me that it is what drew him to MH. After *only one night* with my parents, he said to me, "I really thought you were a decent guy, but I've now met your parents, and it's clear you are underperforming, Boss Man!"

Some of my favorite memories growing up was taking family vacations. It is on these vacations that two of our best one liners came to be family lore. One that sticks out prominently originated because my mom always had a special place in her heart for my brother as a result of the fact that when we were in a terrible car accident, Dick almost died. He had to have several surgeries and my parents felt God spared his life. Dick was also the nicest of the children. And so, on one of our vacations, we four kids were in the back seat being extremely annoying to the two adults in the front. Finally, Dad had enough of our behavior and reached into the back seat to get our atten-tion. All we remembered was Mom blurting out, "Don't hit Dick!" Dick's three siblings interpreted the statement to mean, "Hey, do what you want with Felicia, Mel or John, but by all means, 'Don't hit Dick!'"

Another of my favorite memories are the multiple times I grabbed one of my sister's fingers while she was sleeping and yelled out the famous words "Pick my nose with your finger!" The sheer horror on my sisters' faces was worth the price of admission.

My parents were very traditional—my dad was a general practitioner and my mom a nurse who decided to be a stay-at-home mom. Mom's one cuss word when she would get mad at Dad was when she called him "Clyde" instead of "Honey." I'm sorry I had to tell you this; it was a very bad word to her. Her traditional behavior wasn't just limited to her clean vocabulary. In fact, when our home was broken into, the first thing she said was "I'm glad the dishes were done."

Mom loved the St. Louis Cardinals baseball team, and she and Dad were at Busch Stadium when the Cards won the championship in 2006 against the Tigers. Still, out of all the great Cardinals over the years, there was one who stood alone: Albert Pujols. She loved Albert like no other. In fact, Dick and I wondered if, when she told people she had two sons, she meant that one of them was Albert and either Dick or I were out! Even when Albert went to the Angels, Mom would continue to cut out clippings of how he was doing. Many, many years later, I bid on a signed jersey for his Down Syndrome foundation and when I asked him to sign it for my mom, he also, without anyone asking, made her a video thanking her for being his number one fan. I like Albert!

While Dad did well financially, he never wanted to come across as a wealthy doctor on our family vacations. His solution? To have the children use orange crates for their luggage. You read that correctly: orange crates with pictures of oranges brightly painted on the side of the cardboard box. I once had a guy see me carrying my orange crate and gave me a dollar. I didn't bother trying to explain Dad's reasoning to him.

Just how determined was Dad not to splurge? Well, he bought a used camper that slept four—interesting math since we were a family of six! In other words, Dick and I would sleep in the back of the station wagon.

The typical travel day was 11 hours in the car. We only drove for seven hours but spent four stopping by every single roadside historical marker Dad could find. The frequency of these stops took a dramatic turn when his children were able to drive and developed a collective hearing problem where we simply couldn't hear their father say, "Let's stop and see what the historical marker says."

Still, it's worth noting that Dad loved history and the kids ended up loving history. Dad loved God's creation and the kids ended up loving God's creation. Dad also loved opera—and well, as far as statistics go, two out of three isn't bad.

He also taught his children a very valuable lesson in life that involved playing the stock market. The lesson was simple: if Dad bought something, you should sell it, and if Dad sold something, you should buy it. Unfortunately, Dad passed this gift on to me.

Dad also passed on his lack of athletic skills to his children. The crowning achievement was when his boys played Little League baseball. It is one thing to be relegated to the position the worst player would play—right field—but his two sons were so gifted in baseball they actually *shared* the right field duties.

Dad also passed on his belief that life should include good-natured fun. When I was a senior in high school and we first got the pool in our backyard, one day, a few of us guys decided to grab a female friend who was over, carry her to the new pool and throw her in. When we got to the driveway and saw Dad walking into the house, the girl, thinking she had been saved, yelled out, "Dr. Wieland, help me!" Dad looked at us, looked at the pool and quickly ran inside the house. That was strange, but I realized his mission when he came running back out to the pool with the key to unlock the pool gate: he was there to open the door and enjoy the dunking.

Other days, he would play cards and have beers with my high school friends. Before you think he should be retroactively arrested, remember that these were different times.

Many kids find their passion in high school, and I was no different. It's just that my passion was for socializing.

When I was in high school, I got in trouble for shooting the moon. For the unenlightened, this is when you pull your pants down to your thighs and show people your butt—something that in small town Jerseyville in the '70s was considered high entertainment. I planned to do it while driving by the school and word got out, so a crowd of students gathered—whooping, hollering and cheering as we drove by. The principal wasn't as amused (I was easily discovered because we had to make another trip back, this time with me standing in the back seat waving to my adoring friends.)

Mom and Dad were out of town during the eventful day, so I called my dad to share the news. He wasn't thrilled but appreciated the humor. Mom was on the naïve side, so when he then told her that I had been suspended for shooting the moon, she responded, "That's nice, what is a moon?" Once Dad explained, she cried the rest of the trip.

Because I didn't want to flunk or do the work to get A's, I ended up an average student. But figuring out what to do afterwards was easier for me than most because there was only one subject I liked and showed any promise in: math. One of my math teachers in junior high actually told my parents that I was a genius in math. (Later, that teacher completely recanted that statement and said there was a fine line between genius and crazy, and she later leaned heavily the other way.)

Anyway, numbers and I got along, so I knew my occupation would have to involve them. What made math fun for me was that it provided a puzzle to solve and there was always a "correct" answer. A self-study program in junior high enabled me to fly through algebra and geometry in one year. Then I started to get into calculus and higher math classes, and it was like, "Hold it. Back up the bus. This isn't fun anymore." I concluded that I needed something with numbers that didn't include the hard stuff, and accounting fit the bill.

Two things stayed with me from high school. First, typing skills! Being able to type was very beneficial in college, not to mention in my career. The second thing was what I learned from being on the basketball team—the importance of sacrificing for the greater good, the significance of both winning and losing together, ways to get along with people who rub you the wrong way, why minor roles are still very important to the success of the team, how culture goes a long way to determine your success and why, if you put in the time, you will be a better teammate.

You don't need to be on a sports team in order to learn these things. Debate club, band, drama, 4H—any type of a team will provide you the opportunity to learn great life lessons.

Despite my math skills, it's safe to say that I was not interested in education when I was in high school. Let me put it this way: the ACT test is scored on a scale of 1 to 36, and the average score those days was 21. When I took the ACT, I got a 9 in English (now you know why I have an editor). I think my overall score was 17, and then I worked on it and got it up to a whopping 19.

When it came to college, I didn't have a lot of choices. Okay, I had one choice: Western Illinois University; I'm not sure they declined many applicants. When I went to Western, my parents paid for everything. Some people may think parents paying for college isn't a wise decision because a child should have some skin in the game or they won't take it seriously. That is often true, but it had the opposite effect on me: I was paranoid I would flunk out and embarrass my mom and dad. My skin in the game was not money but respect and love for my parents. So even though my first year I drank (a lot), it definitely took a back seat to school and pick-up basketball. I never missed a class; I took notes and I studied hard before tests. I also found out that I could memorize things for a 48-hour period, which was great for content-based subjects. In fact, I ended up with high honors. It really came down to the fact that I loved my mom and dad, knew it was a stretch for them to pay for college for all of their kids and I was not going to waste their money.

I ended up with one C, though not from a lack of effort. It so happens, in English, I am *not* smarter than a fifth grader. Because of my incredibly poor score on the ACT in English, I had to take a remedial English class. I scored 90's on all the tests but when I got my final grade, it was a C. What the heck? There must have been a mistake. I went to the professor to complain, and he told me in a not so delicate way, "Pal, if you had to take this course to go to college, you don't deserve anything better than a C," adding that a C was the top grade he gave. I think he also told me I shouldn't tell other professors I had to take that course because it would affect their overall opinion of me. He had a point.

In the end, I got five great things out of my four years at Western Illinois: I embraced the Gospel of Jesus Christ, met Julie, received a good education, passed my CPA on the first try and played a ton of basketball.

And Mom and Dad didn't get on my case about the C; they made it clear that we were smart enough to pick our own grades. They made that point to each of their children. If there's one thing they maintained, it was consistency. When Mom's twin sister went through a divorce and decided to go back to school, my cousins Mike and David came to live with us for two years. I assumed that Dick and I would still get treated like their sons and Mike and Dave as nephews visiting. WRONG. If we got new clothes, Mike and Dave got new clothes. If we got disciplined for misbehaving, so did Mike and Dave. Basically, Mom and Dad treated them exactly like their own kids. They also loved them like they were their own.

These experiences influenced me so much that now Julie and I widely open our home to people. Four of their grandkids, Mike, Chris, Nathan and Nick, spent many days (and nights) at Mom and Dad's house growing up, and even though they all had fathers, Dad was another father figure to them. Each of them credits Dad for showing them a great example of what it looked like to be a responsible man.

While we each gave our parents a certain amount of heartache, Melanie admits she won that contest. There were times when she could have easily been voted off the island. Oh, I forgot, she actually *was* voted off the island in high school for a few years when Mom and Dad felt they had to get her away from the crowd she was running with and sent her to Wisconsin. She spent years and years struggling with narcotics, going into rehab three times and even attempting suicide—something she's open in public about because she knows it helps other people who are struggling. And yet, when it came down to our parents' last chapter of this life on earth, it was Melanie that was the rock star. This is the beauty of God's Grace and redemption. She served and honored our parents.

It was hard to say goodbye to our Dad. And saying bye to Mom three years later was even harder. Dad had been ready to meet his Savior for several years, but Mom still loved life, her friends and her family. When you lose your first parent, you still have a parent. When you lose the second parent, you become an orphan. Nobody wants to be an orphan, even if you are 60.

Mom's final weeks were difficult. Melanie lived with Mom and Dad during each of their final days. We all had been trying to pitch in, but Melanie and Dick were definitely the "A" team. A few weeks before Mom passed away, Felicia and I told Melanie and Dick we would help Mom get up to go to the restroom. As I lifted Mom up, I stepped on her feet and the only thing Mom did was look at Dick with that expression that said, "Why don't I have the 'A' team here?"

It is a lot harder to live the gospel than preach the gospel. Mom lived out the gospel. Mom gave, Mom served, Mom sacrificed, Mom loved. In return, she had joy, love and untold blessings in this life and her life in heaven. People have said Mom was lucky to have such doting kids

and grandkids, that we smothered her with love during
her last days. They got it backwards. Ours was just a token
response to how Mom treated her kids and grandkids
every single day of her life.

When Dad died, we mourned. Mom mourned, but she
continued to live. As a widow, with stage four ovarian
cancer, she spent a week in Australia, along with me and
300 other people from different companies on a trip spon-
sored by one of MH's suppliers, where she climbed the
world-famous Sydney Harbour Bridge. All anyone in the
group seemed to talk about was my mom and how she
climbed the bridge when others decided not to because it
was too dangerous. When countless people came to talk to
me and Mom, I was reminded yet again of who the
popular one was!

Mom's faith grew deeper over the last 10 years of her
life. She struggled for years as she tried to decide if she
was good enough to earn heaven. Reading the Bible, she
realized salvation has nothing to do with our good works
but with what Christ did for us on the Cross. In the last
few decades of her life, she realized she would never be
good enough, but Jesus was. She found peace.

Dad was not perfect. He suffered from depression and
low self-esteem at times. He had a hard time controlling
his desire to buy art, especially Western art. He had a hard
time not buying presents for my mom (though I guess
that's not much of a weakness). Dad was just a guy who
truly gave his wife and children everything he had.

All of us are still works in progess, and we swing and
miss on what we should do. But each of the four kids

developed two strengths from our parents: a measure of grace towards people and a belief that we should try to do the right thing, simply because it was the right thing to do.

Mom instilled in those around her the art of grace and mercy. Dad instilled in those around him the art of "you do the right thing because it is the right thing to do."

They did teach us a few other things over the years—that you love your spouse with your whole being and that you never give up on your children or friends, even when everyone else has.

"You got lucky, John."

Yes, I did.

CHAPTER 2

FOUR ADOPTIONS AND ONE ABORTION

When Julie and I got married, we decided to wait a few years before we had kids. But eventually, we started trying to have kids.

No luck.

We decided to go to the doctor and see what was up. To make a long story short, Julie had some issues, and I had some issues. It seemed like everything would have to be aligned perfectly for us to have biological children. We did artificial insemination with no luck.

To be honest, going to the hospital for the artificial insemination was one of the most embarrassing things I've ever done. The way it works, of course, is that the male's semen is collected in a container before being placed strategically in the female's uterus. This sounds pretty benign, but when I went to do my side of the equation, they had me go into the bathroom, where they put a sign on the outside of the door that said "Semen specimen in process." How do you look someone in the face when you come out of the bathroom carrying a cup and having to take that sign off the door? Where is the sense of privacy?

It did eventually become clear we were probably not going to have any biological children…which brought me back 12 years earlier to when I was in high school.

It was my senior year. Plans to attend college were in place. The world was before me and it felt like there were endless opportunities. I was dating a classmate during my junior and senior years in high school—a comfortable relationship born of hormonal passion during that time in my life—and it wasn't long before she became pregnant. I didn't feel either one of us was in a position to get married, let alone have a baby, and the idea of having the child and giving him or her to one of the million couples who cry out to God for a baby to adopt didn't even enter my mind. At that time in my world, life was simple: it was all about me, whatever was best for me at that moment. So, at that time, we made the decision to have an abortion. I don't know how much I pushed, but I do know I was in favor of it. I also believe if I had been in favor of having the baby and pushed toward that decision, there is a very good chance we would have had the baby.

Thirty-eight years after the abortion, the girlfriend I had gotten pregnant reached out to me on Facebook. We both decided that it was important to include our spouses in the correspondence and through the messages that followed, we were able to communicate things that we were either too young or too stupid to communicate previously.

I told her my memory was that I paid for the abortion.

She had different memories.

I remember you telling me you had plans for college and that we were too young.

I remember being at the abortion clinic, sitting on a bean bag chair in the waiting room, waiting for them to call my name.

I remember the pain of the procedure.

I remember sitting in a recliner after the procedure feeling numb and cold and empty. Looking around wondering what I had done and wondering if I would go to hell for taking this soul's life.

I remember seeing you for the first time afterward. I remember not wanting to be intimate.

I remember you saying it was important "for me" to have intercourse again so I would not be bitter.

I remember you going off to college that fall.

Not a month goes by that I don't wonder what my child would have looked like, what my child would have become. I count my child as one of my own. My oldest. I had a ceremony for my child's death. I pray for my child's soul.

Significantly different memories, wouldn't you say? Please take a moment to reread her comments. Let her words sink in.

While excruciating on some level, she told me that these conversations helped in her healing process—that a choice made at such a young age was not easy or simple for either of us. And it helped me, too—by helping me to see how God brought beauty out of ashes in both of our lives.

Twelve years after the abortion, I was being told, "John, you are not going to have any biological children." The irony and sadness did not go unnoticed. The only biological child I would ever have I aborted, terminated, killed, sacrificed—whatever your vernacular would be on this subject.

Because of the abortion, I had a fair amount of self-hatred during that time of my life. In a perverted way, I thought this simply served me right. But God is rich in mercies, and we adopted four newborn babies, each with an interesting insight and unique beauty.

———————

Julie began working with the Department of Children and Family Services for five years in 1985. While most people working there either get burned out or jaded, Julie embraced her job as a ministry and service to God, and that made her able to stay enthusiastic.

One day in late 1989, she learned that a girl in one of the families she was working with was pregnant. While the girl had been working with an adoption agency, she really liked Julie and so she asked Julie if she'd like to adopt her baby when she delivered.

Julie and I were excited—really excited, beyond excited —and told our friends and families about the great news. Then, when the delivery date grew closer, we did not hear from the girl. The due date came. We did not hear. One week went by. We did not hear. A second week, still nothing.

Finally Julie called to see if everything was okay. That's when she learned that the girl had decided to go with the adoption agency she had been working with. We understood; the adoption agency had a lot invested in this pregnancy and didn't know us from Adam and Eve.

But we were devastated.

Our family and friends joined us in our misery. They knew we really wanted to be parents. Still, we took the high road. We told our family and friends, "If God wants us to have a child, He can make it happen." What a mature and godly testimony we made to our faith! Yet my heart was nowhere close to what my head was thinking or my mouth was saying. I knew my words were true, but my heart was a wreck.

And then, two weeks later, on January 30, 1990, I was at my office when I got a call from a doctor friend of my dad. He said, "I delivered a beautiful baby girl last night. Would you and Julie like to adopt her?"

It really was that easy for God to give us a child. I immediately said yes, feeling like this was one of the few times it was okay to make a decision like this without talking first to Julie.

I decided to surprise her and so I told Julie that we needed to get down to Jerseyville because Grandpa Robertson was sick. That evening I asked her, "Hey Julie, if we had adopted that one baby and she was a girl, what name would we have given her?" Julie didn't want to chat about babies and names; her emotions were still pretty raw. So I decided to tell her. "Julie, we are not going down to Jerseyville because Grandpa is sick," I admitted.

She immediately asked, "Did Grandpa die?"

"No, honey," I responded. "We are going to Jerseyville to pick up our baby daughter."

Julie broke down and cried. We named her Jessica Leigh as an homage to my dad, whose middle name is Lee.

Our second child, Jennifer, came to us in just as surprising a way.

It all started when Julie met a pregnant woman, "Jane," in the fall of 1992.

Jane already had one son, but as a single mom, two would be more than she could handle, and so we made arrangements to adopt her daughter once she was born. Things were progressing nicely—Jane and her mother loved Julie and they seemed committed to placing this child with us at the time of delivery. We met everyone in Jane's family—her mom and dad, her grandma, the biological father and her son.

When the big day came, Jane and her mom asked if Julie would like to go to the delivery; they actually let Julie cut the umbilical cord! The next day, we stopped by, excited to see our new baby. But when we arrived at the hospital and saw Jane sitting with her mom, looking incredibly uncomfortable, we knew something was amiss. Jane finally said, "I don't know if I can go through with this."

Once again, Julie and I said all the right things: "Jane, you have already done the right thing." "You have given this baby girl life." "Whether you raise her or we do, you have already won."

We were kind and gracious, but when we left, we were broken—another perceived addition to our family taken away at the last minute. Her mom asked us to come back the next day—explaining that by then Jane should be able to figure out what she wanted to do.

Sunday after church we went to the hospital again. Jane

and her mom were there, looking a lot more peaceful than they had the day before. We exchanged greetings and Jane told us she had made up her mind; then she went on to another subject. Jane's mom exclaimed, "Jane, tell them what you decided!"

Smiling, Jane said to us, "I really want you guys to have this baby!"

The following day was 72 hours after the birth—the earliest you can finalize an adoption. Jane and her mom wanted to meet us at St. Mary's Cathedral, a beautiful church in Peoria. There at that altar, we held Jennifer as our very own. We gave her the middle name Esther for Queen Esther of the Bible and also because Jane's grandma was named Esther.

This was our one "open" adoption, and Julie and I were honest with Jane. We told her that we would love to provide updates and pictures and even early visits, but after a year, it would be too complicated. We knew that if Jennifer had her biological mom involved in her life, it would be very confusing for Jessica, and we were not willing to risk how that might play out. Jane understood.

On March 10, 1992, a little over three months after Jennifer was born, we got another call from Dad's OBGYN friend from Jerseyville. The call was similar to the previous one: he had delivered another baby girl and wanted to know if we would be her parents.

I struggled, not because I didn't want this baby girl, but

because I knew there were millions of couples dying for just one baby and now, we would have three, with the last two just months apart.

"Did you know we adopted a baby just three months ago?" I asked.

"I did," he said, "and I don't care. I want to place this baby in a home where a family will love her and I don't care if that family has no children or five."

We don't deserve another blessing like this, was my thought. That's when I realized that many of us have a skewed opinion of God. We think God will bless us but that He has to balance it out with bad things; we believe that we only deserve several blessings and not an overflowing cup. *If I got three good things in my life*, I was clearly reasoning, *then God would be obligated to push a few bad things my way*.

Why do we as humans want to put limits on His blessings? It's like me saying, "Okay God, I know You wanted to bless us with Jessica and Jennifer, but another baby girl? You need to stop these blessings! They are over the top." Pretty silly logic, isn't it? I quickly came to a conclusion: God does not keep a record of good and bad things to average out. If God for some reason wanted to bless us beyond measure, well, bring it on. We called the doctor back and said we would love this baby girl. We named her Jamie Elizabeth.

Raising two daughters who were three months apart was just like raising twins, but one of the best decisions we made was to separate Jennifer and Jamie as they entered school. We knew it was important for each of them to make their own way, have their own friends and develop their own stories.

I loved having daughters, but people often asked me if I wanted a son. I would always answer, "I guess, but I am perfectly happy with my three girls." And I wasn't blowing any smoke; I felt completely whole with Jessica, Jennifer and Jamie. I think that is a little bit of how God works. We really don't miss something we have never experienced.

On November 25, 1997, Julie got the call from Dad's friend again: this time he had a biracial baby who needed a home. You may be thinking: *this doctor must have quite the business placing babies into adoptive homes.* In truth, he doesn't. I believe he had three babies to place with a loving family, and he placed all three with us. He liked and respected my mom and dad. They would socialize together. And really, is there a better way to tell someone "I like you" than to give them grandchildren?

This time, Julie didn't think *she* needed to consult *me*. She said yes. We held Josiah for the first time as our own the day after Thanksgiving. Is it any wonder that Thanksgiving is my favorite holiday?

The other kids, being kids, didn't understand what a big deal this was to us. When we went to church that weekend and saw some of our friends in the hallway, I told Jennifer, who was five years old at the time, to share our big news. Rather than announcing the arrival of

Josiah, she blurted out, "Tomorrow is my birthday." Classic!

When we went to the courthouse to sign the papers, Josiah's birth mom said she wanted to talk to Julie but not me. Ouch! Julie asked why she didn't want to meet me and she said, "Why would I? The mother does everything!" Our experiences sure affect our worldview.

Raising Josiah helped me to evolve even more than raising the other children had. I knew there would be challenges the other kids hadn't had simply by virtue of the fact that he would be growing up biracial in a white community. Then, roughly 10 days after we had adopted him, we found out his left eye was underdeveloped, and he would probably have no vision in that eye. My concerns about race evaporated right then, and I started to think about the challenges he would have without vision in his left eye.

Then we discovered that he had severe asthma—so severe that there were nights Julie or I would be holding him, just praying to God he wouldn't die. My concerns about him not having vision in one eye evaporated, and all I hoped for was that this little guy would live. It is fascinating how life circumstances help us put things in proper order.

We never let Josiah's eye be an excuse for him to not do or try anything. In fact, I told him as he grew up that not having vision in both eyes would be a big thing, but not having vision in one eye was a little thing, so he was lucky that he only had a little thing to overcome. When he got older, we had a plastic lens painted and placed over his eye so the sides of his face would be symmetrical.

Josiah ended up becoming all-state in soccer—the second leading scorer of all time in our soccer-rich school. He led the soccer team to the Elite Eight his junior and senior years and was the point guard in basketball when his seventh and eighth grade teams went to state. He scored 37 points in a basketball game as a freshman and was the point guard who went 28-3 his junior year. He then received a soccer scholarship to play at Taylor University and led the team in goals his junior year and total points his senior year. If you saw him play anything, you would call me a liar if I told you he didn't have vision in one eye.

Instead of being a victim, Josiah chose to overcome his challenges. He is a hero to the parents of the few young kids in our community who don't have vision in one eye because he shows their kids that they don't need to be held down.

———

Julie and I didn't have many conversations on the subject of whether we would tell our children about the adoption stories.

We told them from the very beginning about their own individual adoption story, consistently explaining that their biological mothers were rock stars—that no one would go through nine months of discomfort, sickness and pain for someone they didn't really love. I've heard esti-

mates that out of 100 women who get pregnant acciden-
tally, only one goes through the birthing process and
places the child with a family. I think that is a definition of
a rock star. We explained that to go through all that for the
sole purpose of giving their baby a better opportunity in
life than they felt they could give is a great example of love
and sacrifice.

We also told them that we were open to any of them
reaching out to their biological mom or dad after they
turned 18. We have never been insecure about this possibility; we understood that there's not a finite amount of
love in this world—that if the kids met and loved their
birth parents, that wouldn't mean they would love us less;
it just meant there was more love in their life. But setting
expectations was critically important. We wanted the kids
to have only one expectation: to tell their birth mom,
"Thank you for giving me life and I will always love you."

Of course, even if our children had the appropriate
expectations, we don't know what the expectations might
be of their biological mothers. To date, only one of our children has reached out to meet their biological mom.

As we look back on the beauty of our adoption stories,
Julie and I thank God we didn't have any biological
children.

CHAPTER 3

PREPARE THE CHILD FOR THE ROAD, NOT THE ROAD FOR YOUR CHILD

As my parents raised me, they assumed that I behaved like they did. I didn't. Losing my virginity before high school and starting to drink at the same time did not prepare me for a moral life. Because of my parents' grace to all people, I was never a bully to anyone, but I sure was very narcissistic: in high school, all I focused on was girls, alcohol and basketball.

My one true regret is my rudderless pursuit of sex when I was young. When you are a young person pursuing sex, it's limited to two things: the visual and physical aspects. This set me up to be shortchanged on what sex could be. Sex is designed to not just be visual and physical but also mental, emotional and spiritual. When those five senses come together, sex is an incredible gift. Even though I try to bring the mental, emotional and spiritual into the marriage bed, because of my past, the visual and physical are still the dominant focus.

So if my parents raised me thinking I would behave like them, guess how I raised my kids? Yes, thinking they would behave like me. Therefore, I became a helicopter parent. Julie not so much. I was very guilty of preparing the road for my children: if there was a difficult curve coming up, I would work the road so it was only a slight turn. Thankfully, my kids have turned out to be good-hearted people in spite of my interference.

If I had been more focused on preparing my children for the road and not the road for my children, I would have been less concerned about their happiness and more concerned about their character. Happiness is a momentary emotion—the root word, in fact, comes from "happenings." Character, on the other hand, is the essence of who a person is; by developing a strong character, they will have joy and contentment in life.

There were a few times I parented well. Once, when my daughter Jessica was a freshman in high school, she stole $50 from my billfold. I typically didn't keep much money in my wallet, but for some reason that day I had a $50 bill in there. I went to work out, and when I took a shower and got dressed, I realized the $50 was gone. Jessica was the only child at home, so it was pretty clear who took the money. Jessica denied, denied and denied—and then, somehow, the money ended up back in my wallet.

I finally said, "Jessica, I know you took the money, you know you took the money and God knows you took the money. Just be honest about it."

She finally said, "I put it back!" I guess that is a confession!

I wasn't mad at all. I sure had my problems growing up, so I could relate. I asked Jessica, "How many times do you have to kill someone to be called a killer? How many times do you have to lie to be called a liar? How many times do you have to steal to be called a thief? Jessica, you don't want to be considered a thief, do you?"

She understood and I asked her to recommend a punishment; we ended up with something much less severe than her recommendation.

When your kids fail or make mistakes, it's important to understand that these are teachable moments. It's better to be more concerned about the development of the child than the severity of the punishment. There are a lot of opinions when it comes to disciplining your children. Some believe we should be having rational conversations with a three-year-old and let the child decide what is the best course of action for them, while some believe a severe butt whoopin' is required for the most minor of offenses. Others have beliefs in between.

Growing up, my mom's weapon for punishment was simply the disappointment on her face. Sometimes she would have tears in her eyes, and sometimes she would have a stern look, but the sad face was always most effective. I could be terrible to just about anyone growing up, but when I made my mom sad because of my behavior, I would feel like a complete jerk.

When my dad disciplined, he would use his hands or, once in a great while, a belt. I don't remember getting a spanking from Dad very often, but I do remember the last time he tried to whip my brother and me. My family was in Colorado for our annual family vacation trip to the YMCA in Colorado Springs. Dick and I were, for some reason, throwing rocks at each other (at 13 and 14, not the smartest thing in the world to be doing). I don't know when a parent should quit whipping their kids, but I'm pretty sure it doesn't have its desired effects when they are teenagers. Dick and I were laughing as we were receiving this punishment. That's when Dad concluded those butt whoopin' days were officially over.

When we were raising our kids, Julie gave them "time outs" when needed and a wooden spoon when they were openly defiant. I used "time outs" at times, told Julie to handle it at other times and would give swats on occasion.

One night I was in a bad mood, the kids were going crazy—they wouldn't pay attention—and my temperature was rising. We were all in the girls' room and Jennifer, who was six at the time, accidently pushed one-year-old Josiah off the bed. I laid down the law, giving Jennifer three relatively hard swats. She glanced over at Julie with a look that said, "Why is my dad hitting me?" I saw the look, and it hurt because Jennifer was by far the biggest Daddy's girl of the three in those days. Julie asked why I was so mad.

That's when I had an epiphany. The first swat was for Jennifer's correction, while the second and third were for my personal satisfaction. When I realized that, I apologized to Jennifer and the other kids and told them the truth —that the first swat was to get your attention and potential edification, but any swats after that were for my own satisfaction. I promised if I ever gave my children a swat in the future, it would stop at one. This was a promise kept.

Any type of punishment, whether it is corporal or a time out, can turn from corrective (for the child's benefit and growth) to punitive (corrective discipline plus some more). From that day on, I became much more strategic about any discipline, always asking myself, "What's the least invasive response to help train my children?"

Discipline is for the benefit of the child and not the satisfaction of the parent. Good words to remember!

I learned a lot about life and myself while raising children. But they weren't my only teachers.

———

What can I say about our dog Molly? Well, she was dumb (a better word might be "psychotic"), had bad eyesight, barked at everyone and would go to the bathroom in the house. Still, she was discerning, never peeing on any of our wood floors and instead seeking out the rooms with carpet.

Molly had issues with storms, and when thunderstorms came, she would compulsively bite the water supply lines to toilets or sinks. Three different times we came home to find standing water in our basement.

I hated that dog at times.

I would have to remove the basement carpet and pad before having carpet layers put the carpet back in place.

The carpet layers, on the other hand, loved Molly.

One day when friends of ours—a couple and their baby —were living with us for a season, Molly struck again. The husband was at work and his wife, Hannah, and their baby were alone in the basement. Hannah heard people talking upstairs and then heard something hit the floor, followed by footsteps. When she couldn't get ahold of her husband, she called me. While our neighborhood is very safe, I raced out of work and called the police. When I got home, I asked Hannah and her child to leave the house through the basement door. When the police came, they searched the house and Molly ran out to be with me. The police asked me to come in and discuss the caper. We checked a few hiding places, and then the police took me to the front room where, in the middle of the room, was the signature of the bandit: a nice pile of dog poop! On the carpet, of course.

We concluded that someone must have called our house phone and left a message, which was the talking Hannah heard. Molly then reacted to that by breaking through the gate, which is what Hannah heard hitting the floor. The footsteps Hannah heard were from Molly running around like crazy. Yep, crime solved and the culprit had four legs. I believe there were a total of five police officers at our residence and they left giggling and smiling.

One day I left Molly in the garage for a few hours, and when I came back, the garage was a complete wreck—everything knocked over, including a plastic gas can, which had left a small circle of gas on the floor. Since no one else was home, I had to clean up this mess and decided to first take care of the gas on the floor. There are many ways to remove gas from the floor: you can put sawdust or compound on the gas and then sweep it into a sack, you can remove it by using rags or you can simply put a match to it. (Did you even know that was an option?)

I always felt if you have a job to do, try to get it done quickly. So I went in the house and got a match, figuring it would burn for a few seconds and then die out. I lit the match and threw it on the gas, and it started out just like I planned. But I didn't realize that there was another puddle of gas under some items that were knocked over and the other puddle was *five times as big* as the visible puddle. Big mistake. I was now in the middle of a healthy garage fire— and the garage was also attached to my house. I tried to separate the things on fire. The plastic gas can, now on fire, had melted a hole on the top of the container with about three gallons of gas. I'm not a fireman, but I knew that was a problem.

I was able to get the gas container out of the garage, but there was still a healthy fire that didn't seem to be dying out. I took off my dress shirt, hoping I could swat the fire out, but that just increased the flame. I figured I was completely screwed, but then I remembered that we had a fire extinguisher in the house.

If I only knew where.

I actually found it on my second guess.

Then I thought, *Now, if I only knew how to use it.*

Fortunately, it was self-explanatory, and I was able to bring this unfortunate event to a close. The damage added up: one plastic gas can, one step ladder, one power washer, the power cord for the generator—not to mention any shred of ego I'd had. I took as many of the casualties as I could to our burn pit to destroy the evidence, but the smell was too great to keep this quiet.

You may be thinking that I am an idiot, but you are missing the point.

It was Molly's fault.

All of my family and friends would side with you on this issue, but I held a grudge against Molly since that fateful day.

Later that autumn, Julie and I went to a movie, and we left Molly outside with her wireless fence collar. Molly loved to be outside. When we got home a little after 11, it was raining and Molly was nowhere to be found. I spent the next two-and-a-half hours looking for her in the rain, driving to other neighborhoods, rolling down my window and calling out her name as loud as I could while still respecting those sleeping at that time of night.

My heart was beginning to sink as I thought, "Where is she? What is she doing?" I knew she was afraid. I had heard stories of dogs being able to find their way home even from hundreds of miles away. Maybe Molly will find her way home, I thought. I decided the best thing to do would be to get some sleep and then recruit other family members and strategically search within a five-mile radius in the morning.

Sleep eluded me. I kept wondering where she was, hoping she was okay and alive. At 3:30 am, I thought I heard something and sat up in bed to listen more closely. Yes, that was definitely a dog bark, and it sounded like Molly. I threw on my my robe and ran outside. There was Molly, wet, cold and shaking in the cul-de-sac. She wouldn't come into the yard because she knew she would get shocked if she crossed the electric fence. So I went to the cul-de-sac, picked her up in my arms so she was high enough off the ground to avoid any shock and carried her into the house. I got a towel and dried her fur, holding her and kissing her on her head. I said comforting things to her. Once Molly got comfortable, she lay down and went to sleep, and I returned to my bed where I slept with a deep sense of joy.

So why would I respond this way to a dog that has been basically a pain in my butt?

Because she was a well-behaved dog? No.

Because she brought me great joy? No.

Because she didn't cost much money? No.

The reason was simply this: even with all of her dysfunction, she belonged to me.

She was *my* dog.

She was part of *my* family.

She lived in *my* house.

Yes, I loved that dog, despite her craziness.

Then I realized: I may be a dysfunctional person who loves a stupid dog, but what about the love God has for me? God is perfect and awesome. In God's eyes, I am a bigger mess than Molly. Still, He loves us even in the midst of our brokenness and dysfunction.

It reminded me of Jesus telling a story to explain the Father's love for us:

> *There was a man who had two sons; and the younger of them said to his father, "Father, give me the share of property that falls to me." And he divided his living between them. Not many days later, the younger son gathered all he had and took his journey into a far country, and there he squandered his property in loose living. And when he had spent everything, a great famine arose in that country, and he began to be in want. So he went and joined himself to one of the citizens of that country, who sent him into his fields to feed swine.*
>
> *And he would gladly have fed on the pods that the swine ate; and no one gave him anything.*
> *But when it came to himself he said, "How many of my father's hired servants have bread enough and to spare, but I perish here with hunger! I will arise and go to my father, and I will say to him, 'Father, I have sinned against heaven and before you; I am no longer worthy to be called your son; treat me as one of your hired*

servants.'" And he arose and came to his father. But while he was yet at a distance, his father saw him and had compassion, and ran and embraced him and kissed him. And the son said to him, "Father, I have sinned against heaven and before you; I am no longer worthy to be called your son."

But the father said to his servants, "Bring quickly the best robe, and put it on him; and put a ring on his hand, and shoes on his feet; and bring the fatted calf and kill it, and let us eat and make merry; for this my son was dead, and is alive again; he was lost, and is found." And they began to make merry.

Now his elder son was in the field; and as he came and drew near to the house, he heard music and dancing. And he called one of the servants and asked what this meant. And he said to him, "Your brother has come, and your father has killed the fatted calf, because he has received him safe and sound." But he was angry and refused to go in. His father came out and entreated him, but he answered his father, "Lo, these many years I have served you, and I never disobeyed your command; yet you never gave me a kid, that I might make merry with my friends. But when this son of yours came, who has devoured your living with harlots, you killed for him the fatted calf!" And he said to him, "Son, you are always with me, and all that is mine is yours. It was fitting to make merry and be glad, for this your brother was dead, and is alive; he was lost, and is found."[1]

Many people refer to this parable as the Prodigal Son. The word "prodigal" has several meanings; one of them is "reckless or extravagant behavior." The son? Millions have walked that road before. The Father's Love, Grace and Mercy? Now that was reckless and extravagant behavior. A better title would be the Prodigal Father.

CHAPTER 4

WHO IS YOUR NEIGHBOR?

As children we learn from our parents in many ways, but the most effective is when we see our parents respond to life. Many of us have heard the phrase "lessons are caught, not taught." There is a good bit of truth in this statement.

I learned about the concept of loving your neighbor from my parents, and the first time Julie and I consciously acted on it was when, newly married, we met a couple named Keith and Brenda in our Sunday school class.

They were an interesting couple. Brenda looked very athletic but was really uncoordinated. (She played catcher in slow pitch softball and had to roll the ball back to the pitcher because she couldn't throw it within five feet of the pitcher, which qualifies as a little uncoordinated.) Keith, on the other hand, didn't look like an athlete—he was short and a wee bit chubby—but he was a scratch golfer, and in all my years playing basketball, Keith ranks in the top three in being able to score from anywhere on the court.

But when it came to Keith and Brenda, what I appreciated most was their authenticity. Most "Christians," when their home life is blowing up before their eyes, will tell their friends, "Things couldn't be better." Keith and Brenda actually told the truth—a novel approach to life.

Keith was trying to make it as a salesperson in a tough industry while Brenda stayed home with their growing family. Keith drove some junky, trashy car with hundreds of thousands of miles on it. I drove junky, trashy cars as well. I don't borrow money for cars, and I'm not the tidiest person in the world. When someone in the back seat asks if those are actually my sweaty socks on the floor...well, I think you have a visual. I also didn't know how to maintain a car. In fact, when my dad gave me a car for college, I didn't change the oil for 40,000 miles. That is how much I knew or cared about cars.

Keith needed a car.

I had a powder blue Taurus that had 200,000 miles on it that was worth only a few hundred dollars. I decided to upgrade and get a new "used" car, and Julie and I thought we would offer the Taurus to Keith. The fact that Keith would accept this offer tells you all you need to know about how broken down his car was! Thirty-five years later, after Keith and Brenda had moved to Indianapolis, become financially successful and been driving really nice cars for years, they came to my 60th birthday party and reflected on their time in Peoria, bringing up this small act of kindness. Over the years, they've given their cars to missionaries instead of trading them in. This is the beauty of being a good neighbor; typically, when you are a recipient of kindness, you look to pass the kindness on to others.

I'd first learned about being of service to others against my will when it came to my dad's relative—a second cousin or something named Jenn. She was really old and lived in an assisted living facility in the Alton, Illinois area. Every Christmas, Dad would drive to Alton and bring her to our house for the day. She couldn't hear or see very well and had really thick glasses, so when we played cards, she was always playing the wrong card. My siblings claimed she was cheating and simply acting like she was playing the wrong cards by mistake.

The whole Jenn thing required a lot of effort; just

driving to get her and back took two hours. One time I rode with Dad to take her home and on the way back I was telling him how stupid it was to spend holidays with Jenn. I added, "She cheats at cards!"

I went on for a little bit before Dad blurted out, "That is enough, John!" Then he said, "We are the only ones. If she's not with us, she sits in that room by herself every holiday. Now tell me John, what would you have us do?"

I was silent the rest of the way home and after that Jenn didn't seem like such a pain. The rest of the kids and I actually enjoyed playing cards with her and felt blessed by the opportunity to be with her on holidays.

I still think she cheated at cards, though.

I also learned about service through my grandpa on Dad's side. He might have been a little bit of a hypochon-driac: he was convinced that he would be the first sibling to die in his family, but he actually outlived all seven of them. He also always walked with crutches; whether or not he actually needed them is a topic for another day. The last few years of his life, for some reason, Grandpa wanted to go to the bank on what seemed like every Saturday. He didn't drive at that time, and since I was a 16-year-old with a license, I was chosen to be his chauffeur.

This weekly routine included me helping Grandpa get up from his chair, out the door, into the car, to the bank, out of the car, into the bank and into the office to sit and wait and then do the same thing in reverse order. Of course, I would then complain to Dad about how I was the one always having to do this.

Dad made it clear to me that you honor your elders, especially your grandpa. He told me that this was the right thing to do and that there would be a time when I looked back on our trips with a smile and a warm heart. Boy, Dad ended up looking like a prophet. Even today, my heart is warm when I think of my trips with Grandpa.

But sometimes when we serve others, it doesn't go the way we think it should go. Julie and I have had dozens of people live with us from time to time. When we were first married, she worked for the Emergency Response Service of Peoria where her job was basically crisis intervention. Depending on the situation, Julie would either go into a setting by herself, ask for the police to come or be called in by the police. It was risky business, especially when emotions were high, but her department and the police did a good job of coordinating and assessing the situations to mitigate the risk.

It was at this time that Julie met Andy, a man in temporary need of housing who had been a client but had progressed within the system to be part of the staff. Andy was a broken and lost soul, both because of the hand he had been dealt and because of choices he had made.

Julie, living out the concept of "Who is my neighbor," asked if I would be open to Andy moving into our house for a while. Because of my upbringing and how Mom and Dad opened their home to people, I had no issues with it. So Andy moved in with us, sleeping on a couch in our basement. We all ate dinner and watched television together at night. We even let him use our cars when he needed to get out of the house or go do something.

Then, after living with us for about a month, Andy started to steal from us. We confronted him about it, but he didn't stop, so I finally had to tell him that he had broken trust with us and would need to leave.

A few days later, he abducted a lady in downtown Peoria, took her in her car to the countryside and shot her in the head, leaving her for dead. Miraculously, she survived and wasn't even seriously injured because the bullet glanced off her skull.

Andy was caught and convicted and is spending the next 99 years in federal prison.

The formal charge read like this:

On April 21, 1987, an incident occurred in Peoria whereby a woman was confronted as she was getting into her car by a man with a gun. The defendant was later identified as the man with the gun. Defendant forced the woman to the passenger's side of the car and drove east out of Peoria. Defendant stopped at a gas station and forced the woman to buy gas and cigarettes. They continued driving, and at some point, defendant pulled over near a ditch. Both of them got out of the car and approached the ditch. Defendant made the remark that the ditch was not deep enough, and they got back into the car and continued driving. About a mile or so further, defendant pulled off the road by a barn or shed. Defendant walked the woman behind the barn while telling her she could run away when she saw the taillights of the car disappear. The woman testified that defendant ordered her to stand facing the barn with her palms against the wall of the building. According to the woman, defendant fired the gun, and the bullet struck her in the left wrist. She screamed and fell to the ground. She pretended to be dead, hoping the man would go away. However, a few seconds later, she heard a gunshot and felt the bullet hit her head. Again, she heard a shot, and a second bullet hit her head. She lay there for some time, still conscious. Eventually, she got up, crossed a field to a farmhouse, and received help. Her wounds were treated that night and the next day surgery was performed to remove metal fragments from her head.

Defendant was later apprehended in Denver, Colorado. The woman's car was recovered there also.

This raised some serious questions for Julie and me. Why didn't Andy steal everything he could from us? Why didn't he ask to use our car and then just take off, never to return? Worse yet, why did Andy choose to shoot a stranger and not us? All we know is we thanked God the lady who was shot made a quick and complete recovery.

People ask us if we regretted ministering to Andy, and we always say no. The way people respond to us when we serve them has little to do with our actions. That is their decision. God is honored when we serve, regardless of how the person we are serving responds. So often people get tied up into the response they get, but the only thing we can control and will be held accountable for is our own choices and behavior. It is never wrong to do the right thing, and so we press on in serving others. If we had stopped using our home to serve, my wife and I would have missed out on the incredible blessings we have received over the years.

This reminded me of the interesting conversation Jesus had about neighbors.

And behold, a lawyer stood up to put him to the test, saying, "Teacher, what shall I do to inherit eternal life?" He said, "What is written in the law? How do you read?" And he answered, "You shall love the Lord, your God, with all your heart, and with all your soul, and with all your strength, and with all your mind; and your neighbor as yourself." And he said to him, "You have answered right; do this, and you will live.

But he, desiring to justify himself, said to Jesus, "And who is my neighbor?" Jesus replied, "A man was going down from Jerusalem to Jericho, and he fell among robbers, who stripped him and beat him, and departed, leaving him half dead. Now by chance a priest was going down that road; and when he saw him, he passed by on the other side. So likewise a Levite, when he came to the place and saw him, passed by on the other side. But a Samaritan, as he journeyed, came to where he was; and when he saw him, he had compassion, and went to him and bound up his wounds, pouring on oil and wine; then he set him on his own beast and brought him to an inn, and took care of him. And the next day he took out two denarii and gave them to the innkeeper, saying, 'Take care of him; and whatever more you spend, I will repay you when I come back.' Which of these three do you think was a neighbor to the man who fell among the robbers?" The lawyer said, "The one who showed mercy on him." And Jesus said to him, "Go and do likewise."

Who is your neighbor? Open your eyes! They are right in front of you.

CHAPTER 5

I'VE GOT YOUR BACK

As I mentioned earlier, when I was growing up, my cousins Mike and David lived with us for a few years. Mom and Dad treated them no different than their own sons. One day when Mike was in high school, he heard a few boys were going to gang up on him after school the next day—he was a very good athlete, but being the new kid at school and having to defend yourself against more than one kid was terrifying. He told his Uncle Clyde what was happening. Dad didn't say a whole lot about the drama, but the next day he left his medical practice, went to the high school, confronted the kids and told them it would be a fair fight. Those boys wanted no part of Dad, left and never bothered Mike again. When Dad was in his final chapter of life, Mike called to chat, and I asked him if he remembered that incident. Mind you, this is over 50 years later. Mike said he remembered Dad coming to his aid like it was yesterday.

I always wondered why Mike would still remember this small incident with my dad. The answer came when I was talking to my two oldest nephews, Mike and Chris. They are twins who were very good football and basketball players. I was only 18 years older than them, so when they were in their late teens and 20s, I was still relatively competitive in basketball. The rough and tumble games we played at my parents' house were almost legendary, like the time I pushed Mike off my back on a rebound, causing his arm to go through the garage window and require 20 stitches.

Mike and Chris grew up in a divorced home and spent a lot of time at my parents' house. When they were about 10 years old, they came to Grandpa and Grandma's house from the movie theater. I was in my late 20s and visiting that weekend, so I noticed that both Mike and Chris looked like they had been crying. After some questioning, they finally told me the story: a 14-year-old boy named Dylan had roughed them up for no apparent reason other than the fact that they were walking through an alley, and this bully decided to have some fun at their expense. The moment they told me the story, I bolted out of the house, drove uptown and found Dylan outside a Dairy Queen sitting on his bicycle. (Yes, he was on a bicycle.) I walked over, grabbed the bicycle, put him and his bicycle on the ground and told him if he ever touched those two boys again, he would have to deal with me. (This definitely was not one of my finer moments as a 29-year-old man.)

I came back home with mixed feelings. On the one hand, I'd defended my nephews. On the other, I'd defended them by threatening a 14-year-old child! The other adults—Julie included—made it clear they thought I should be arrested and asked me what I'd been thinking. I did calm down and decided they had a point, so I went back to Dairy Queen and found Dylan, still on his bicycle. (Again, he is on a bicycle and I'm 29!) I went over and apologized for scaring him so much. Evidently, I didn't scare him too much because he looked at me and told me to eff off! I was truly a confused individual.

But Dylan never messed with the boys from that day on. Thirty years later, as I was putting thoughts together for this book, I asked Mike if he remembered that incident. I thought he would say no. He looked at me and said, "I remember it like it was yesterday."

Two stories of young boys coming from broken homes, and they remember someone who had their back.

CHAPTER 6

DIFFERENCES ARE WHAT MAKE THE WORLD GO ROUND

Since I just told you about what a good guy I was for defending my nephew, I need to confess I have irked him and his brother plenty.

Mike thinks things always turn up roses for me. The reason he may have that belief is I tend to brag every time something goes my way, and it gives the appearance it always happens. On the flip side, I can be pretty silent when things don't go my way!

One Thanksgiving weekend we were at my parents' home, and Mike and Chris were visiting from Carbondale along with their wives, kids and dogs. On the Wednesday before Thanksgiving, Chris' dog Bougs ran away. Bougs is a mutt—honestly, there's nothing special about that dog other than the fact that his owners love him. Mike and Chris and their families spent most of the day looking for Bougs but couldn't find him.

After Thanksgiving dinner, they went out looking for him again. They were getting increasingly worried and started calling friends to see if anyone had seen him. There were rumors of a dog being seen west of town and then north of town. On Friday, they decided to continue the search, and I offered to use my tracking experience of zero to help the cause. I took my parents' car. *If he started out on the west side of town and went to the north side of town*, I thought, *I could head him off at the pass on the east side of town*. This was my brilliant detective mind at work.

Traveling east of town, I decided to take a country road for no apparent reason and saw a dog about a half mile up the road. *You're kidding me*, I thought. *That cannot be Bougs!*

As I got closer, I discovered that it was actually Bougs. Think about it: Bougs could have been anywhere within 10 miles of our house and I bumped into him in less than 10 minutes.

I stopped the car, called his name, picked him up, put him in the back seat and took him back to the house. Needless to say, Mike and Chris were ecstatic. Then Mike asked who found him and was told, "Uncle John did." In exasperation, he laughed and said, "There will be no living with him now!"

I think Mike would rather have Bougs lost than give Uncle John something to brag about yet again.

A few weeks later I gave Bougs a Christmas present: an 8 1/2 x 11 glossy photo of Uncle John, with the words "To Bougs, Your Savior!" Yes, it is tough living with Uncle John!

In a family, everyone has relatives that are different or unique. In my extended family, we have learned this lesson: celebrate and enjoy uniqueness and don't get tied up in little personality defects. Life is short.

Actually, everyone has acquaintances in life and business that are a lot different than they are. Just ask Stan Butler.

It all started when I was chosen to attend the very fine institution named Western Illinois University in Macomb, Illinois.

I majored in accounting in the same class as someone who is now a well-known businessman in Peoria, Stan Butler. Stan is a smart guy, and he was a smart guy at Western. I think he got one B in his entire college career. Stan and I, along with two others, took a CPA review course at Illinois State University on Saturdays. Every Saturday, Stan and the other two would talk about accounting on the way over. I slept. The teachers taught and Stan listened. I struggled to stay awake. Stan and the guys discussed the day's review on the way back. I slept.

There was a problem during this time. Stan and his future wife Cathy had been dating for a long time and had a mature relationship. I had just fallen in love with Julie, and every moment of the day I was either with her or thinking about her. I was running on empty, and it showed during this period of my life.

In May of 1980 we all went to Champaign to sit for the exam. You would think they could come up with a fancier word than "sit" for such a prestigious test. I do a lot of menial stuff while sitting.

Anyway, Stan drew the short straw and had to room with me the night before the exam. Stan was fully prepared; lights out at 9 pm for a good night's sleep. Unfortunately, Stan only paid for half of the room, and on my side, the lights were on and there was a party going on till three in the morning. Books were flying, notes were being scribbled and cries of despair heard. Stan was not appreciative.

We took the exam and Stan felt he did fine. He had prepared well, he knew what he wanted and after the test, Stan felt pretty confident he had done his best. I, on the other hand, decided I shouldn't sleep so much. I came out of the test looking like I just got run over by a bus. I was dazed and confused.

We received the results about four weeks before the awards ceremony in Chicago. At that time, you had to pass each of the four parts with a minimum score of 75. Actually, they don't give scores between 70 to 74. If you land in purgatory, they will either push you down to a 69 or up to a 75, depending on how you did in the other sections. Therefore, if you get a 75, you know you probably didn't get a 75. Stan's lowest grade was in the low 90s, a perfect example of someone that has their act together and goes out and accomplishes their goal.

I was hoping to pass at least one part, as coming up with goose eggs would be a little embarrassing. I received the letter and to my surprise, the first word was congratulations—I got a 75, 76, 77 and an 88. I passed! The whole thing! Just like Stan!

Naturally, I couldn't wait to see Stan in Chicago. The CPA Awards Banquet was held in the grand ballroom of the Conrad Hilton on Michigan Avenue in Chicago with over 1,000 attendees. At the hotel I finally found him, and he stood there in shock.

"Wieland, what are you doing here?" he asked.

"Stan, I passed!" I said. "And my certificate looks just like yours. I guess you studied too much, Stan."

Funny how people respond so differently to the same event. When Stan saw me it was the only time he ever questioned the existence of God. For me, it was a moment that I realized how God shows Grace!

Stan and I ended up in Peoria for most of our careers. For a short time we worked at the same accounting firm. Our paths started to cross more often through Rotary. Even though Stan loved the arts and I leaned more toward sports, we really did get along well. The neat thing about this relationship was that we became fans of each other. I respected his discipline and planning and Stan appreciated my free spirit. We celebrate our different styles and approaches to life.

Life Lesson:

There are multiple roads to success and different definitions for success, and there are different types of people with different personalities that achieve their success. Your way is not *the* way. It is *a* way and just happened to work for you. Embrace and learn from people that don't think, look or act like you. You will be better!

CHAPTER 7

A CHRISTIAN AND A MUSLIM MEET AT THE AIRPORT

In 2014, when Josiah was 16 years old and going to England with his high school soccer team, I signed on as one of the chaperones. My primary responsibility was to make sure Josiah and I had valid passports. Before the trip, I checked twice, and both were valid.

On a sunny Friday morning, the team took a Peoria Charter Coach bus from Peoria to Chicago, arriving with plenty of time for our flight. Josiah and I were at the end of the line, and when it came time to process our tickets, the agent looked at me and then asked us to wait. He came back and informed me Josiah's passport had expired. I had misread the date! How do you explain to your 16-year-old son that his dad is an idiot? Actually, I didn't have to because I believe Josiah offered that up as a possibility.

As the rest of the team left for England, Josiah and I went into downtown Chicago to try to get a passport and new airline tickets (Chicago is one of the few cities in America where you can get a passport the same day). We got him a temporary passport and spent the night in a Motel 6, which Josiah called "very sketchy," and he wasn't wrong: two police cars sat in the parking lot all night.

The next morning, we were able to get the tickets changed about 45 minutes before the plane was scheduled to leave. As we approached the ticket counter, I noticed that the airline employee behind it was dressed in full hijab while I was wearing a "Jesus" shirt. There you go, a proud Christian needing help from a proud Muslim. You could feel the tension at that moment. I handed her our passports and waited for her to process our tickets. She looked at them and then at her computer before handing the passports back. "There are no tickets for you on this flight," she said.

I was now officially screwed. I asked her to look one more time because we'd been told they were there 15

minutes earlier. A little put off, she looked again and said, "Yes, now I see them, but you will have to go through the other line to get your tickets." The other line had about 20 people in it. There was no possible way I could wait in that line, go through security and get on the plane in time.

So I told the lady my story; how I messed up my son's passport, how the team left us behind, how we'd spent the previous day getting him a temporary passport. I told her if I had to go wait in the other line, we would miss the flight again. She was noticeably perturbed but told us to put our passport in the machine. I was grateful for her help even if it was a bit unwilling, and I thanked her for her kindness. My opinion of this lady was improving quickly.

But the passport machine wouldn't work, and when I told her, she looked less perturbed and came around her counter and got it to work for me. I thanked her again for her kindness and meant it with all my heart—I knew how unusual it was for an airline employee to come out from around the counter. She had our tickets in her hands, and I thought at best we had a 25 percent chance of making it through security in time to make the flight. But she looked at me with my Jesus shirt and my biracial son and said, "Follow me!"

This Muslim lady with her hijab took us to the very front of the security check and told them we had a tight connection and to please let us through immediately. I was almost crying because of her kindness, so I reached out, touched her forearm and said, "I really thank you for your kindness." The lady in the hijab received the kind touch on her forearm and only said, "I could have been kinder."

There you have it. I had a bias and she had a bias, but we both got past our biases and learned a valuable lesson. The beauty of two people, two faiths, experiencing the joy of being kind to each other, regardless of their faith, color of their skin or anything else. I won't forget this lesson. And I always remember the Muslim in the hijab.

CHAPTER 8

JERSEYVILLE, WHERE A LOT
OF WHITE PEOPLE LIVE

In 2015, my preacher friend asked if I would host a pastor from Michigan. Jim had started an organization called 95 Connect for pastors of churches with less than 100 members to help them with training, research and encouragement, and there were approximately 250 pastors coming to Peoria to be encouraged and trained. I was happy to help.

The day of the conference, Jim called me again. A pastor from Ferguson, Missouri (yes, *the* Ferguson, Missouri) had shown up unregistered and was planning to drive the three hours back home before returning to Peoria the next day. When Jim asked if I would host him as well, I readily agreed. The two pastors came to our house where Julie and I sat and talked with them.

Bob, the pastor from Ferguson, was black, and one of the first things he said to us was, "Thank you for having me in your home. I am surprised you would let me stay at your house. You don't even know me, and I'm a black man to boot." I responded that we were both followers of Jesus, which made us brothers, and that he was always welcome in our home.

Because I'd been fascinated by what had happened in Ferguson with Michael Brown the year before, I asked him all about it. Bob told us that Michael Brown was a troubled kid with a capital T. In small towns like Ferguson and my hometown of Jerseyville, the community knows who the troublemakers are. But if a troublemaker attacked a police officer and got shot in Jerseyville, I would feel sad for the family of the boy, but I wouldn't burn down my city. When a response to a situation is more exaggerated than the response warrants, there has to be an underlying issue.

And so it was in Ferguson. Bob told me that people knew Michael Brown had big issues and was a bully, but there was an underlying issue of how the police in Ferguson treated the black community. Even our president at the time, Barack Obama, made overtures that the grand jury should convict the officer. But when the grand jury came back and said the police officer was innocent, it started to bring light to what had really happened that unfortunate day. Those who saw the events evidently had a different recollection when under oath.

Bob told us that the few years before the Michael Brown incident, things in Ferguson had changed a lot. The former chief of police had welcomed Bob and other leaders into the station to sit and chat about issues and work together. Then a new police chief came in, a white guy, and he told Bob he couldn't come to the station anymore because he was busy. Bob felt that chief of police started pushing officers to give more tickets, and the community, including Bob, started getting harassed for moving violations.

So when the Michael Brown incident hit the fan, some people from Bob's congregation wanted to protest the police for jacking them around. Bob said, "Sure, but be respectful and peaceful." He told us that the real problem was the people shipped in from God-knows-where, since it was the out-of-towners and not the residents who started to burn down the city.

So the riots were a perfect storm—police jacking around with the residents they were supposed to protect and then some outside group coming in to create havoc.

I shared with Bob my concerns about racism when it came to Josiah. I know I have been able to give my son a lot of life wisdom, but one thing I have never been able to provide is what it will be like as an adult male of color in this country.

Bob said, "Josiah is not going to have huge problems being biracial; light brown skin color is generally more accepted." He continued, "But when you're a dark black man like me, racism is alive and well."

I told Bob that I had asked Josiah when he was a junior in high school if he had ever been discriminated against and he told me he didn't think so. I asked Bob for his take on this and he responded, "Josiah may have been discriminated against and not even known it because he isn't looking for it." He explained that when you are black and your grandpa is telling you the stories of back in the day, you are simply going to have your antenna up. This means that sometimes you might mistake something as racially motivated because you're expecting that when it actually had nothing to do with race.

The conversation with Bob got me thinking more about issues of race. Jerseyville was 99 percent white—maybe 99.9 percent since we could name the families of color in our town...all three of them. Mom and Dad did a good job bringing us up with the understanding that people are people, *period*. Even though we all have biases—even some we are not aware of—I felt rather color-blind growing up.

One of the few black people in my town was my age. His name was Ricky, and he roughed me up when I was in seventh grade. I did not like *that* black guy! Three years later, after I'd gotten my black belt, Ricky joined a Tae Kwon Do class I was teaching. He still scared me a little. My fear had nothing to do with the color of his skin and everything to do with how easily he had kicked my butt a few years earlier.

I didn't see what discrimination looked like until 1975, when I was a junior in high school. I was on the basketball team and considered a defensive specialist (this is code for "I can't throw a basketball into the ocean"). A black family had just moved to Jerseyville, and one of their kids, Marcus, joined the team mid-season. I was pretty confident that if you were a black guy, you were going to be a better player than a white guy. Well, guess what? Marcus wasn't any better than me. In fact, I might have beaten him one-on-one.

Marcus was a good guy, and when most of the players would come hang out at my house, he fit in well. And at school he finally got to suit up for a game. One day, we were either winning by a lot or losing by a lot so everyone got to play—except Marcus. I thought it was odd until I was walking to the locker room and the coach came up to me and said, "I showed him who's boss."

It was ugly. Plain and simple. In my mind I called that coach a jerk, an MFer, an SOB, an AH…you get the idea. My first experience would be considered minor in some circles, but it doesn't make it less ugly. It was ugly, plain and simple.

After my conversation with Bob, I asked a friend I knew from the board of our kids' school, Marty, about his experiences as a black man. Marty had received military training, become a pastor and started working with the Peoria Police Department on racial issues. He has a slender build, is in good shape and dresses well. Let's put it this way, if he sat in on an executive meeting at MH and someone came in to talk to "the guy running the show," they would probably assume it was Marty. He just carries himself well.

I had never heard him talk about racial injustice.

But when I asked him, Marty told me that he has experienced racism personally and that it still exists today, but his personal relationship with Christ has changed how he responds to it.

He shared a story with me about having an interracial relationship while he was in high school and how the white high school counselor had told him to break things off. Marty went home and shared that with his parents. His mother, strong in her Christian faith, told Marty to follow his heart and not pay attention to the counselor's advice. Marty's father had a completely different response: he told Marty in so many words that white people couldn't be trusted and that they were not his friends.

After serving a couple of years in the military and returning back home, Marty saw that his father had given his life to Christ and had healthy relationships with white people. Marty asked his father why he'd responded negatively when Marty had asked him for advice back in high school. His father said that he was trying to protect him and prepare him for the real world as a black man. Marty's dad began to share some of the heinous acts of racism that he had experienced growing up in Mississippi as a black man before the civil rights movement and how that had shaped his thinking about white people.

When Marty saw how Christ had begun to change and heal his father's heart from the evil experiences of racism, it motivated him—and continues to motivate him—to advocate for healing and reconciliation through Christ when it comes to the sin of racism.

He told me that despite being a well-respected member of community, there were times he'd been profiled and stopped by the police department for driving for no apparent reason other than the color of his skin. Instead of continuing the divide, he believes that God used this as an opportunity for him to become an advocate for repairing community relations between the African American community and the police department.

Most people in America would say racism is wrong, and when we see a clear example of racism, it is easy to call it out. But what about the hidden biases, the more subtle forms of racism most of us don't even know we are guilty of? In the late '70s and '80s, when symphonies were called out for biases, they began to hold blind auditions to remove any possible bias based on age, sex or color. If only all of life was so simple.

The black poet Claudia Rankine told a white man asking her about reverse racism, "I have no power over you, so whatever I say to you or about you is not racism. Racism is about power." I take great exception to the quote. Racism is a matter of the heart; oppression is about power. If a group of people has power over another group of people, there can be oppression. But racism and hatred are feelings all groups of people can have.

As a white guy in America, when I go to get a job, I talk to a guy like me. When I get promoted, it is from a guy that looks like me. When I ask for money from a bank, it is from a guy that looks like me. This, no doubt, has bene-fitted me. But there are a lot of white guys that are on food stamps, too. There are also increasing numbers of people of color succeeding in business and owning successful businesses.

I believe racism and discrimination will always exist. It has been part of the world since Genesis. But my great hope is that as our families and friends become increas-ingly multiethnic and multiracial, the presence of racism will diminish. I know that the male I love more than any other male in my life—Josiah—has a black man for a biological father. How could I love my son and not love his DNA?

My nephew, Chris, married a Latina woman from Bogotá named Caroll. I love Caroll and their children, Daniela and David. I love her heritage. And when we do life with people of a different amount of pigmentation— when we *really* do life—we realize that the pigment of the skin has nothing to do with anything.

PART II

BUSINESS

In this section it will become clear how my family as a child and my family as a parent has significantly influenced my values and principles in business. Think about the lessons I just shared:

1. I learned how to win together, lose together and sacrifice for the greater good. Business will always be a team sport.
2. I learned I got lucky to have parents that loved me and tried hard to be good parents. Being responsible for others is the ultimate privilege, and we need to give it our all.
3. I learned through my adoptions and an abortion that there are incredible consequences for our actions and incredible beauty in grace and mercy. Grace is needed in business when you

interact with employees, customers, suppliers and community.

4. I learned that character is more important than happiness in life and business.

5. I learned that discipline is necessary in order to help adjust behavior and not to be punitive.

6. I learned you love people (and dogs) because they are part of your family. This translates to your work family.

7. I learned the beauty of loving my neighbor, even if it doesn't end the way you want. Doing the right thing is never wrong. Doing the right thing in business doesn't always pay off either.

8. I learned that people need to know you have their back when things get tough.

9. I learned to appreciate different personalities, even if they are a little odd…like mine.

10. I learned that biases need to be held in check in life and in business.

11. I learned that racism is ugly. It has no place in a community nor business, as you will see in the next section.

My hope is these principles and life lessons will jump off the page in the next section, as you recognize their impact in how I view and approach business.

CHAPTER 9

A SAFE PLACE

Learning from others has actually been one of the keys to my success. This is especially true when it comes to a group of guys I get together with every month—Chuck, Nate, Andy, Bill, Win, Terry and Mike.

The group started when, at the age of 37, I joined Young Presidents Organization, also known as YPO. I'll admit that when I was first asked to join, it took me a little to get over the name. It seemed pretty self-promoting—not only are we young, but we're also presidents! But once I got past that, I realized it was a really good organization.

The best part for me was the forum group, which consists of about eight people. The key element of the group is TRUST, and three words are repeated at the beginning of each monthly meeting about confidentiality: NOBODY, NOTHING, NEVER. Groups like this take all different directions; ours focused a little more on life issues than business issues, while others may be the opposite. The point for me was having a place to go where I could be honest with my thoughts, struggles and personal failures without feeling judged or fearing that information would leave the room. Trust and honesty are very close bedfellows. You really can't have one without the other. And creating a safe space takes time.

I have been out of YPO for a long time now, for an obvious reason: I was born in 1958, so you can do the math. But our forum continues. As a leader, it is so important to be with a group of people who are not impressed with you and what I will call Baloney-Baloney.

This is the actual form we use as we navigate the afternoon's meeting. Each member completes this form.

Forum Meeting

Reminders

- Confidentiality: Nobody, Never, Nothing
- Safety: This is a Safe Place!
- **Vulnerability** together with **Transparency** increases **Intimacy**, which ultimately builds **Trust**

Check In: One or two words—no speeches, two minutes maximum.

- What is your *ENERGY* level?
- What is your *FOCUS* level?
- Is there anything preventing you from being fully present?

- Mental
- Emotional
- Physical
- Spiritual
- Spouse/significant Other

Issue Clearing: This is where members have an opportunity to address an issue with another member with them. This helps keep small things small things.

   Update Sheet: Each member goes through the sheet below with a six-minute time limit.

MIQ (Most Important Question)

If I could work and focus on **one issue** in my life today in forum, it would be:

Winning Achievements of past 30 days

(not every column will have one)

Business	Family	Spouse	Relationships	Private Self

Challenges of past 30 days

(not every column will have one)

Business	Family	Spouse	Relationships	Private Self

Upcoming Issues or Challenges:

Business	Family	Spouse	Relationships	Private Self

I need help, thoughts, prayers with:

Any updates to a past topic you have discussed recently with the forum?

A **Neat or Exciting Thing** is:

"I notice…" Time: This is where others make observations regarding updates.

Discussion Prioritization

Check Out: Biggest Take-away from today?

It's not that the format is the be-all, end-all of forums, meetings or relationships. It is just an example, and I know that I have grown as a person because of my relationships with those in my forum. There are people that may say, "Yeah, I have that kind of relationship with my spouse, a close friend at work, a very close friend or a sibling." I say: that is great, and you are lucky.

The main point of a forum or a special relationship is to create a safe place to address things in your life so you can be a better spouse, parent, boss, employee or friend. I have a long way to go in becoming the person God wants me to be, but this group of friends has helped me immensely along life's journey. There's perhaps no better example of how they've helped me face some of my less-than-savory characteristics than with what we can call "my very own arch nemesis."

CHAPTER 10

MY VERY OWN ARCH NEMESIS

When our children were in school, I spent a lot of time taking my kids to after-school activities. They were involved in everything from soccer and cheerleading to baseball, basketball, music and drama; the list goes on. And whenever we dropped our kids off, we'd notice that most parents would park in the area designated for parking.

Everyone but Archibald.

No, Archibald would park his car close to where the people were so they could admire his car, which by the way, was a *Rolls Royce*! He would park by a fire hydrant if necessary—anywhere people would see that he was *somebody*.

Archibald didn't even have that great a job, but he sure was proud of his car. He also walked around in a full-length fur coat—even when it was 80 degrees out! He desperately wanted to be known. How phony, I would think. The arrogance!

One day I was at my forum group where I was ragging on Archibald. I knew my financial station in life was exponentially greater than Archibald's. I was more of a "somebody" than him. Yet, I told the group I was humble: I drove a modest car and parked where the "common folk" parked. I got my clothes from Walmart. I did my Christmas shopping at the Dollar Tree!

The guys pressed on my indignation at Archibald. They asked me, "Do you want to be known?" In a brief moment of transparency, I said, "Yes, I want to be known. But in a much more humble way. I want to go places and not be the center of attention, but when I leave, I want people to talk amongst themselves. 'Do you know who that is? He is John Wieland! He is really rich, gives a lot of money away in a very private way and is one of the humblest people in the world.'"

One of the guys said, "Okay, John, let me get this straight. Archibald makes no bones about the fact that he wants to be known and is transparent about it. You, on the other hand, want to be known, but you pretend like you don't!"

Whoops! Houston, we have a problem.

The group decision was unanimous: *I was more of a phony than Archibald.* At least Archibald was honest about his intentions. Johnny-boy was not. I started to realize why Jesus said, *"Why do you see the speck in your brother's eye when there is a log in your own eye? You hypocrite, first take the log out of your eye and then you can see clearly to help take the speck out of your brother's eye."* [1]

Why would Jesus be so in-your-face? I believe it's because we judge people based on their worst examples, yet we judge ourselves on our best intentions. Actually, George W. Bush gets credit for saying this. Good for him.

There's another thing the human heart does to us. The natural tendency is to want justice on those that break the law or worse, transgress against us. But when we break the law or transgress ourselves, we want and expect mercy.

From that day on, I looked at Archibald differently. He turned out to be a nice guy and gracious person.

Without my forum group, I would not have seen how my heart hid safely behind my self-righteous judgment of Archibald.

CHAPTER 11

WELCOME TO MH EQUIPMENT

After graduating from college, I was hired as an accountant at Commonwealth Edison in the Quad Cities. But Julie was in Peoria, and I wanted to marry her more than she wanted to marry me. So, after a year and a half, I moved to Peoria and landed a job with the accounting firm now known as KPMG. Because my experience wasn't overly impressive when it came to public accounting, I was hired at an entry level and took a 20 percent pay cut. This was a good lesson for me: you shouldn't be afraid to take a step back to take several forward.

I loved being a public accountant with KPMG, where I was exposed to new places and people every few weeks. I was a generalist, meaning I was a jack of all trades but a master of none: I audited construction companies, manufacturers, schools, banks, distributors and hospitals. I loved it all and got to see the traits of companies who were making money as well as the traits of those that were not. I was able to talk to CEOs and CFOs and learn how business did and didn't work.

I grew up believing that owning a company was for a select few. Owners of businesses had to be special people who were smarter than everyone else, right? Wrong! One great lesson I learned from working at KPMG was that many owners who seemed to be very successful were not as smart as I thought they would be—some, in fact, were far from the sharpest knives in the drawer. This brought me a level of confidence to go for it. I remember thinking, "They are successful, they ain't very smart. I ain't very smart either, so maybe I can do it, too!"

Eventually I went to work for a well-known local businessman named Tom Spurgeon who owned a business called Lincoln Office. Lincoln was a great place. A lot of people know Tom Spurgeon, and fewer people know me, but those who know us both got quite a chuckle out of that combination. We were definitely the odd couple: Tom is a master of social etiquette, and it has taken me five minutes to figure out how to spell "etiquette." He bought me shoe polish, cringed every time he looked in my messy car and, when he bought his first Lexus, got to hear me congratulate him on buying his Lennox (which is a brand of furnaces, by the way). And while I still need shoe polish, and my team at MH still cringes when they look in my car, I do now know the difference between a Lexus and a Lennox. But I learned a lot more than that from Tom—the main thing being that if you're going to do something, do it with excellence. He also taught me to keep personal and business expenses separate and that real teams can fight like dogs and still respect and like each other. Tom was so generous that he allowed several employees to be minority owners in the company, using the company profits to service the debt. It didn't take a genius to figure that this was a great deal.

When I worked at KPMG, I spent six years auditing MH Equipment, which I quickly learned was a material-handling dealership that had launched in Peoria, Illinois in 1952 and had expanded to include branches in East Moline and Danville, Illinois as well as St. Louis, Missouri. Their main product was forklift trucks that pick up pallets of material or other products and move them to storage racks or other places, and their primary lines of revenue were selling equipment and parts, servicing equipment and rentals. They were virtually bankrupt at the time, but I always thought that with greater effort and capital, they could be successful.

MH had been a nice and profitable business until 1979, the year the company made the decision to get into the aerial work platform rental business—equipment like boom lifts and scissor lifts to lift people into the air so they can work on the sides of buildings. MH hadn't been in this business before and decided to go *big*, purchasing $2 million worth of rental equipment. Life is about timing, and this was a great example of how timing can kill you. In early 1980, interest rates rose to 20 percent and the economy plummeted. So, MH was sitting with $2 million of rental equipment not being rented and paying interest on $2 million at 20 percent.

It's easy math: $400,000 in interest expense, $400,000 in

depreciation expenses (based on a five-year depreciation schedule) and less than $20,000 in rental revenue creates a massive loss for several years—the kind of loss that transitions a healthy company into one that's on life support. Then in 1985, MH's primary supply partner, Hyster, compounded the problem by taking the St. Louis market away.

From 1989 to 1993, about six groups made a run at buying MH Equipment. Many of them had a good plan, but there was one problem: Hyster would have to write off hundreds of thousands of dollars in loans they had given MH Equipment, and they were not ready to do it. So all of these groups were rejected and MH continued to languish in the minutia of continued losses, increasing their negative equity. For those of you who have never (barely) passed the CPA exam, negative equity is a technical accounting term that means a company has more debts than they have assets—in other words, the company is up a creek without a paddle.

In late 1993, Ron, the CFO of MH, contacted me and said Hyster appeared ready to pull the trigger. I was interested in going for it with the money I'd received from Lincoln Office. Ron was correct; Hyster was ready.

Why Hyster agreed to proceed with me is a mystery. Think about it. This proposal came from a guy who was 35 years old, with not only zero mechanical skills but also no ownership skills when it came to running a company. Still, Hyster wrote off $750,000 that MH owed them, gave me $250,000 in incentives and approved my plan. Common sense didn't add up on this transaction. I tell people I was in the right place at the right time, and God is Sovereign.

So there I was owning a company with three branches and 50 people but still losing money. What happened? Simply put, I got lucky! In 1994 the country started a five-year expansion of incredible growth. Just like a bad economy will expose every wart and mistake in a company, a good economy will cover up a lot. As a new owner, I made plenty of mistakes, but I learned from them and the economy gave me time to figure it out. I also had some fully supportive, long-term employees who had been fighting to keep the company alive.

Our CFO, Ron, basically ran the show after Hyster took St. Louis away from MH. The current owner knew he had probably lost the company and would walk away with nothing. Therefore, it was tough for the owner to be all in during those days. I couldn't imagine the stress on him every day. I've never been in a place where my company was going bankrupt, so I have no idea what I would have done. Ron was the guy who held the company together during the last few years prior to 1994; in fact, he was part of one of the groups that tried to buy MH. Ron stayed and supported me for a few years after I purchased MH and then moved with his wife to Las Vegas for family health reasons. Brad, who I worked with at KPMG, and had also helped me on the MH audits, agreed to replace Ron. It was a perfect fit.

Becky started in the accounts payable department many years earlier—1975 to be exact—and her career is an example of why we love America. As the company grew, it became clear we needed a human resources department. We decided to call it the Employee Services Department, and Becky became a department of one. She hadn't gone to college, let alone college for human resources, but she consumed anything she could to educate herself in this field.

Becky and my CFO, Brad, had big titles for a pretty small company. But as we grew, we did a good job of meeting the demands a larger company brings. Becky deserved this ever-growing position because of her pursuit of education, loyalty to our company and a work ethic few emulate.

When Becky took the job, I told her she had one thing to do: keep me and the company out of court. With Becky's guidance and her compulsion for documentation, we have never been in court for wrongful termination or any discrimination. I believe the two things that differentiate MH from other companies is the executive team and the culture. I set a direction for our culture, but it was Becky and her team's job to make sure we lived it.

Another long-term employee was Charlene, and she was in charge of our operating system, which was used by a lot of Hyster dealers at the time. When team members got together to discuss opportunities for improvement, she had the reputation for being the smartest person in the room.

Early on, I ended up with some great hires. This included Randy, our regional sales manager from Hyster, who had vast knowledge and experience from having been at Hyster for 16 years.

Randy would be a great addition, but MH made only $35,000 in nine months in 2014, which equaled $4,000 a month. Yet in October of that year, Randy said he would leave the security of Hyster to become the branch manager of our Danville office (which was currently the armpit of all branches in the country). What was he thinking? Turns out he may have known more than others.

Over the years, Randy has had the single greatest influence on the operations of our company. In fact, my nickname for him for a long time was "The Golden Boy." (When other executive members accused me of playing favorites, I had to quit calling him that, at least in public.)

As we started to grow, I wanted Randy to come to Peoria and run operations, but his son Michael was still in high school, so he wasn't about to take him out of school during his last two years to move to Peoria. I said, "Okay, I'll wait." A week later, Randy called to tell me they were ready to move. I asked him, "What happened?"

He said, "I told Michael why we weren't moving, and Michael said, 'Hey, let's go!'" In other words, because of Michael, I got Randy to Peoria two years early, where Michael met his wife Trisha and ended up giving Randy and his wife Candy three grandchildren. Talk about a win-win-win!

Randy works independently, seeing ways to make our company better and then simply making the company better. When people ask me what he does, I usually say, "It is pretty complicated, so you probably should just ask Randy." This is a much better answer than "I have no idea."

We also hired a salesperson in Danville named Jim, and though he retired in 2020, he was a living legend—thoroughly relentless when it came to knocking on the doors of potential customers. One time I met him at 7:30 in the morning and jokingly asked what he had been doing so far that day. He handed me two business cards that he had received prior to the 7:30 meeting. There were even a few customers who formally requested that he quit harassing them and never step foot on their premises. This became our new standard; if a salesperson hadn't been kicked out of a customer's office for their relentlessness, then they were no Jim. Most customers would simply give up and give Jim what he wanted, which was their service business.

Rest assured, Jim wasn't just an irritant to customers. If he wanted information on a part for a customer, he'd usually wait about two minutes after asking for it. If he still didn't get an answer, he'd accuse whomever he'd asked of not doing their job. In short, Jim was both the most hated and most loved person in the branch, taking us from four technicians when he started to 18 when he retired. His success had nothing to do with me; I was just the lucky guy who hired him.

But at the time I didn't understand that it was luck. When the economy was thriving from 1994 to 1999, and we grew from 50 employees to 125, one person even started to tell me I was a genius (yes, her name was Mom!). It seemed like everything I touched turned to proverbial gold. I even received the Peoria Small Business of the Year Award.

Then, in 2000, Hyster told me they would like to see me grow geographically.

Compliments and praises are great unless you start believing them. I decided, yes, I am a genius, and watch what I can do! To the west of MH was a pretty good dealer in Iowa called Iowa Machinery and Supply (IMS). It had three divisions: a Hyster dealership, an industrial supply dealer that sold bits for drills and cutting material and an Ingersoll Rand dealer. On the east side was BGM, which was primarily a Hyster dealer.

I started to negotiate with both dealers. IMS had multiple owners, and our culture appeared to be aligned very well. We kind of had a deal—until Ingersoll Rand said they would not approve MH Equipment as the new dealer because they wanted to make the Iowa area a company-owned store (owned by Ingersoll Rand).

This was a huge red flag, but remember: I thought I was a genius. I figured I could make it work. So IMS took a little less for the company and I lost a third of the revenue. We closed the deal on September 20, 2000.

BGM was a different story. A guy named Rocky was the owner, and we were definitely different. He drove a BMW; I drove a Taurus. He had a Rolex watch; I didn't have a watch. He wore big rings; I wore a modest wedding band. I wanted to buy his company, and he knew it. During the negotiations, Rocky simply kicked my butt all over the place.

It was embarrassing, and I learned a big lesson in those days: if you covet something badly, you are a terrible negotiator. I estimate I paid close to $1.5 million more than BGM was worth. The only revenge I got on the deal was in the final version of the purchase contract, when I required the net equity after all due diligence to be $1.5 million. We closed on the last day of 2000, and Rocky and his attorney said nothing about the language. Once the contract was signed, the equity ended up being closer to $1 million, which meant most of the hold back money went back to me. Rocky didn't like that very much.

If you think I won the final battle with Rocky, you're wrong. I was renting five of his buildings, and when I wanted to buy them, he knew. My terrible negotiating skills when I want or need something kicked in. Overpaid, overpaid and overpaid.

In a matter of three months, I bought two companies and tripled the size of MH Equipment. *Next*, I thought, *the world!*

Things were beautiful on January 1, 2001, but we started to see the market soften and our un-billable time for our technicians increase. When we closed out January of 2001, we had lost $100,000. Being the great leader I thought I was, my response to this huge loss was, "Well, I hope that doesn't happen again!"

It didn't. In February, we lost $200,000. Hope is not a strategy!

After the first six months, we lost $700,000. Note to self (and Mom): I ain't no genius! My ineptitude as a leader could have been legendary if the public knew about MH Equipment and my leadership.

I did absolutely nothing until March when my CFO suggested I may want to do something about the fact that our artery was slashed wide open, and we were losing a lot of blood. Not because I wanted to, not because I was a good leader, not because I was looking to the future, but out of necessity I started to analyze and make cuts and expense reductions—which included reducing my own and other leaders' salaries. I knew that if I didn't act, we probably were not going to make it. I was acting like a victim, not a victor.

That's when I learned some simple questions to ask to determine if I was acting like a victim or a victor:

1. Is hope your strategy, or are you facing the tough realities and analyzing and pursuing all options to be sustainable?

2. Do you complain about the hand you have been dealt or do you accept it and play it the best you can?

3. Do you spend little time taking personal responsibility for your lot in life, or do you take ownership for what you did to create the environment you are in?

4. Do you think your problem is revenue related, or do you create a cost structure that will support the current revenue stream?

5. Do you feel defeated, or do you have the quiet confidence that you will prevail?

I was five for five in the victim category in that period of my life, and only out of necessity for survival did I finally step up, own my circumstances and lead.

During that sixth month, God took me to the woodshed and gave me a paddling. I learned many lessons about coveting, about pride, about having blinders on and about not listening to your wife. Oh, I forgot to tell you: Julie said she didn't think it was a good idea to buy two companies so close together.

I paid an incredible amount of tuition to get that education, but it did pay off.

At the end of 2002, Hyster decided to sell their company-owned dealership in Ohio and West Virginia, with branches in Kentucky and Pennsylvania. The dealership had 250 employees, did $45 million in sales and, most importantly, had lost an average of two million dollars a year. Hyster wanted me to buy it. My coveting days were over, though, and so we prayed about it and decided that if there were any red flags, we would walk. We held our ground, didn't overpay, hired 215 employees to support the current revenue stream and in the first year made $300,000 for that region. I am a much better negotiator when I really don't care if I get something. That is a good place to be.

There were two leaders of this company, and we needed to decide whether they would be part of the new leadership team. When I interviewed the top guy, I asked what issues were causing the company to do so poorly. He proceeded to trash Hyster—their oversight, decisions and pretty much every single thing about a company-owned store (where the manufacturer owns the distribution of the product). This leader took no responsibility for the company failure. I was able to make a pretty quick decision: he was not coming with us.

I interviewed the other leader and asked the same question. He said, "Hyster owning the dealership has its challenges, but there are a bunch of things I could have done better." I knew he was someone I could work with.

During this transition, two of our future owners, Fred and Coit, joined the company. I'd met Fred at adult Sunday school in the early '80s; we discovered that we both liked to play basketball and have been friends ever since. Back in late 1993, Fred was in the midst of a career transition, and we were actually talking about buying MH together: he would run sales and marketing, and I would run operations and the office. Fifty-fifty. Hyster was not moving very fast at the time, and Fred got a great opportunity to work for a company in Cleveland, so that equal partnership didn't pan out. It is pretty clear that it was God's Grace it didn't happen that way: equal owners have a real challenge making things work in the long term. It can be done, but the number of times it blows up is massive.

Fred and I are pretty different. He'll read the details of a contract no matter how long they are; I run out of gas after the first few sentences. Fred likes fine food and socializing with suppliers, whereas I took Fred to Steak and Shake to celebrate his arrival to MH. His cars are immaculate; mine are not. I tend to write in short sentences with simple words; Fred does not! Such differences are necessary in an organization, and Fred did a great job in his areas of responsibility. We both firmly believe that a 50-50 would not have worked for us.

Then there was Coit, who was actually the president of Hyster at the age of 35. During his tenure, I was the chairman of the Dealer Council, and we'd spent a lot of time together. Julie and I developed a relationship with him and his wife Leigh when we all went on awards trips. He was the rising star within the organization—until the day his daughter Haley gave a report in her third-grade class. The subject was "What do your parents do for a living?" When it came time to brag about her father being the president of a big organization at such a young age, she said, "My father travels for a living, and I don't see him very much."

It is amazing how a few words from a nine-year-old daughter can change a career in an instant. Coit decided that was not going to be his legacy, and he and I agreed he would join MH Equipment.

Coit has a presence about him, especially in meetings with the bigger companies. If we had to get a deal, and there was going to be one person with the bat in hand to take the final swing, it would be Coit. Once, we were negotiating with a Fortune 100 company that was looking for a fleet manager. They interviewed fleet programs from the Original Equipment Managers (or OEMs), which is the company that makes the product, like Hyster and Toyota. They interviewed other national fleet providers, but since we were in the same city as their corporate office, they allowed Coit and me to meet with them. We were the last people in, almost as an afterthought. After our meeting, the group of eight people who were conducting the interview decided they needed to strongly consider us. After they interviewed our references for hours—references that included people from General Motors, Anheuser Busch and Con Agra—they chose us. I would say Coit hit the ball well!

When you have such excellent team members, it's crucial that you know how to lead them. And over the years, I've learned some things.

CHAPTER 12

LEADING LEADERS

During the Great Recession of 2008 and 2009, we had to do a fair amount of cost cutting to break even. It was at this time that, for various reasons, I decided to suspend my board of directors. The board was advisory in nature, which means they had no real authority but would give me advice. Back when I bought the company in 1994 and knew next to nothing, bringing in smart people to talk things through was an absolute necessity. But over the next 15 years, MH built a strong executive team that knew the industry and our business significantly better than our board. In addition, by that time, six executive members had become minority owners of the company.

The big question on the table was: could I create an environment where the executive team also served as the board of the company?

"Power corrupts, absolute power corrupts absolutely" are words to remember. Without an outside board, would I be a tyrant? The verdict has been rendered, and I was able to navigate being the CEO and principal owner without stifling the other leaders on the team.

For a leader to lead leaders, I embraced **Seven Principles** that help create a positive and constructive environment. Rest assured, I didn't start out with this list; they evolved as I looked in the rearview mirror.

1. Understand your power begins and ends with the chair you sit in.

Most of us know people that are given some authority and act like they are the most important person in the world, and you are a meager subject of their domain. If they didn't sit in that chair, you wouldn't even listen to what they had to say. It is all about the chair. I understand that; it's why I get the obligatory laugh when I make a stupid joke, why people ask me if I lost weight when I actually gained 10 pounds and why people still nod their heads when I say something really stupid. I get it, I laugh about it, I even make jokes about it. It is just the stupid chair. If I didn't own MH, I would be readily told when my jokes weren't funny or that I was actually gaining weight or that my comment was a demonstration of my ignorance. So when other leaders of MH see me getting undue attention or hollow compliments, instead of feeling resentful, they know I'm smiling on the inside, and they can smile too. It's important to not think too highly of yourself and remember it's just about the chair!

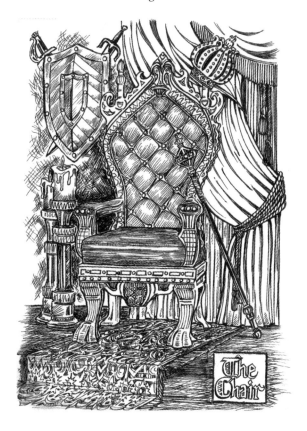

2. Every voice in the room is important.

You may hear leaders say, "Every voice on the leadership team is important." But that doesn't always play out when you sit in their meeting. It's crucial to look at how the meeting flows. When someone is talking and the boss interrupts, does the person speaking stand down? If the boss is speaking, does everyone sit in silence, never thinking of interrupting? If the boss and another leader start speaking at the same time, does the other stand down because the boss speaks? If the answer is yes, it's clear that not every voice is important—or at least not as important as the boss's. A leader of leaders will be very intentional when it comes to deferring to others as much as others defer to them in meetings.

If you are leading leaders, and they feel their voices do not count, you will not have strong leaders on your team. When someone has an idea, the first question I ask myself is, "What is the worst outcome if we do this?" There are many times when the worst outcome is manageable, so if the leader is passionate about the idea, it's better to let them run with it.

One time, Bill, one of the original owners of MH, had an idea about starting a brokerage division where we would buy equipment and sell it to another company for them to try to sell it to yet another company. We had dabbled in the brokerage business in the past with marginal success, but we didn't have a leader own it. Bill felt we needed to go big or go home.

"John," he told me, "we need our own warehouse for this operation."

If this blew up and failed, we would probably lose $200,000. If it worked, who knows? It was not my vision at all—it was all Bill—but I said to him, "Go for it!"

So we bought a building in Indianapolis next to our branch office and started the division from zero. Today it has six employees buying and selling equipment all day long and generates about a million dollars in sales per month. It worked because Bill had passion, competence, vision and trust.

In our business, managing fleets of equipment is

extremely important. Knowing that to be a leader in the field you have to differentiate yourselves from the competition, I asked Coit to run this new division. Jim Collins, in his book *Good to Great*, says, "Put your most talented people on your best long-term opportunity," and I took Jim's advice. (For the record, Jim Collins does not know that we are on a first-name basis.) Coit said he would run it, but we needed our own platform. Once he explained that by platform, he meant our own software, I asked if he was sure. He told me it was required if he was going to take the job. I didn't see the need for the new platform, but Coit is a smart guy, so again I said to go for it. We started with a blank piece of paper and asked ourselves who would be around the table deciding our future and then asking what was in the software specifically for them. We discussed positions like maintenance people, controllers, safety and operations. Ultimately, we ended up with what was probably the best software system in our industry for a period of time, though after a while we started seeing other software solutions that looked a lot like ours. With our passion for fleet management and software that provided great information, we grew this into a new business that grossed over $50 million in a few years.

Neither of these ideas were mine; I didn't even get the vision clearly. But if you want leaders on your team, you have to let them lead.

In addition to listening to their ideas about direction, a true leader needs to have solid ears when it comes to constructive comments about what they are doing. Every time I have talked in public or preached at church, I've prepared a transcript and asked a half dozen people to read it and make comments. The practice has been golden: the final content is always significantly better than the original draft.

Every two years I go to every branch in the company and give a "State of the Union" presentation. In 2020, I drove over 5,000 miles in four weeks and gave the presentation 43 times, essentially living the movie *Groundhog Day.* My goal was to improve after every delivery, and the main improvements were the result of listening to the comments from each territory's executive team.

While the last two presentations didn't change, the other 41 did. In the end, the branches I visited early on were shortchanged, because the final version was head and shoulders over the original. When leaders know you genuinely want their input, they will provide it, and you will be so much more effective in communicating.

I have also learned important or relevant facts can come from anyone—even employees you don't think highly of. Over the years I've had employees that complain, create discord and always think they know what the leaders should be doing. Some of these people have occasionally expressed concerns about our operations, and even though most of the time there's nothing to them, a few times the information they provided was correct. As a result of listening, we were able to make corrections and became a better company.

3. Don't lose leaders because you are greedy.

One of my board members told me, "Never lose a great leader because of money," and there is a lot of truth to this statement. To keep talented leaders, it was important that these leaders not only felt MH was their company but that it actually *was* their company.

In 2003, I brought six of the leaders into an ownership program, allowing them to participate in the buildings we buy through Limited Liability Corporations (LLCs). While our executive salary structure is modest, our bonus program makes up for it; in other words, if the company does well, the leaders do well, and if the company does really well, the leaders do really well. Some of the leaders can make one to two times their annual salary through bonuses! When an owner retires, the company buys back the stock at the time of retirement, but they get to keep their interest in the buildings they have ownership in and rent payments until their death or the death of their spouse, whichever is last.

It is almost counterintuitive. The more that great leaders experience ownership, the more the company grows in strength. To put it another way, 85 percent of 1,000 is more than 100 percent of 500.

As a CEO, the goal is to always be thinking, "How can I get this leader more money?" and not "I wonder how long I can keep under-compensating this leader?"

4. A private offense requires a private apology; a public offense requires a public apology.

I've had private conversations with my leaders that have turned heated and didn't end well. Often, after thinking through what happened, I'd realize that I crossed a line or was insensitive to an issue so I'd go to their office or call to apologize. But if you treat an employee like crap in front of a group of people and then go to that person's office and apologize privately, you are a weak leader and will begin to develop dysfunction in your organization. In fact, if you offended the employee in public, the private apology will make matters worse.

One time when we had an executive meeting in St. Louis, I was in a foul mood and got into it with another member of the team and kept pushing to the point that the leader got up and left. The executive member felt abused, and the other executive team members had no problem letting me know I had been a complete jerk and my actions were unacceptable. If one person thought I was a jerk, I could say that was their opinion. If all of them said I was a jerk, there was not much wiggle room to argue. During a break, I apologized to the employee, and then when we reconvened, I admitted to the entire group that I was completely in the wrong and apologized again to the guy I'd been a jerk to.

Recently, a peer in my industry wanted to know what I was going to do about an MH customer issue. I thought he had the information wrong but told him I would follow up and get back to him. I was correct—he didn't have the correct information, and MH did absolutely nothing wrong (that time!). I called and left a message for him to call me. He didn't. When I talked to someone in his organization, I asked why he didn't call me back. The answer was, "He's not into apologies." That seems a little too convenient.

5. You need freedom to fight.

As I shared earlier, when I worked with Tom Spurgeon at Lincoln Office, we were polar opposites. As a result, we could get incredibly frustrated with each other once in a while and really go at it. But the next day, Tom always treated me like nothing happened. The issue was over, and we had moved on. Great lesson!

One of the great things about a small company is that everyone often wants the exact same thing. At MH, one of our saving graces is that the executive team is truly pursuing the same destination for the company. This comes from having value statements that everyone believes in and that do not conflict with each other. This means that you have freedom to fight over issues, but at the end of the day you are on the same team, wanting the same thing.

A prime example of this is Darrell, one of our executive members who came with us during the purchase of Iowa Machinery on December 31, 2000 and is part of the original ownership group. Darrell and I have a lot in common: we like to talk and give our opinions (even if we don't have an opinion). We are passionate and can get excited. And so it may come as no surprise when I tell you that Darrell and I have had more knockdown, drag-out fights in the executive meetings than all other fights combined. In fact, when we start going at it, other members just lean back in their chairs and smile. This is not a monthly occurrence, but it has happened from time to time.

At one point, I wanted every branch to have a banner

on the outside of their building that showed the employees and how many years they had gone without an accident. I saw this somewhere and really liked the idea. Darrell would have been the one to execute the idea, and he didn't see the genius in it. Finally, he said we had to do the banner at corporate. I explained that there were no technicians there, so the banner wouldn't have a point. He said, "You said all branches, John."

I finally yelled, "Darrell, we just have to do it, and quit trying to shove these banners up my ass!"

Well, that was that until a group of us, including Darrell, went to TGIF and started laughing about my "shove it up my ass" comment. I actually re-enacted the drama. I am sure other patrons thought we were drunk, but there might have been three beers on the entire table. We still laugh about the banners 10 years later. The point is that you can fight, but when it's over, move on.

I do have one rule I work hard to keep. If I criticize someone in a meeting, I will work very hard, as quickly as possible, to compliment them on something or take their side on an issue. Everyone—especially the person I tangled with— needs to know that the issue is over and that there isn't any residual impact. It helps people feel safe defending their position when they know that if we get into it, after it is over, we move on to the next topic, and no one holds grudges or even thinks about it anymore.

6. It's good for the leader of leaders to be the butt of the joke sometimes.

If a leader of leaders is the one person that people don't make fun of because of the leader's response, it creates dysfunction. Of course, there is a difference between being belittled by your team and your team having some fun at your expense. While I've never felt belittled by my leaders, we have all laughed quite a bit at my expense. If I end up on the short end of valor in a meeting, leaders need the freedom to laugh about it.

Once, one of our leaders, Randy, was explaining a new process and was using numbers for examples. Truthfully, his numbers did not make sense (remember, I'm a bean counter). I very seldom go at Randy in meetings; he is introspective and guarded with his words. But for some reason, I wouldn't let up on his bad numbers. Randy finally said, "John, we are talking about a concept, not numbers, so get off the numbers." This was uncharted territory for the two of us, and there was dead silence. Until Bill, who is very quick-witted, said, "Checkmate!" Everyone busted out laughing, including me. When people realize the leader of leaders accepts good-natured fun at his or her expense, everyone should be able to laugh at themselves. But remember, it has to be "good-natured" fun.

7. Play the "We are going to do this because I say so" card about once every five years.

One thing I have learned over the years is that if I have made up my mind on a topic, I should not ask for input because it just confuses everyone involved and comes across as very disingenuous.

Leaders of leaders have to make decisions. When making decisions, it is important for the other leaders to know what type of decision it is and what role they are to play.

There are four main types of decisions a CEO makes:

1. Decisions of low importance.
2. Decisions where you want additional input from leaders before you make a decision of some importance.
3. Decisions where consensus is desired because it affects the entire enterprise.
4. Important decisions where you go against the group.

Let's take a look at each of these.

1. Decisions of low importance.

Actually these types of decisions should occur infrequently and only for expediency; the rest of the time support people should be taking care of them. When a CEO is making these types of decisions on a regular basis, the perception is that he or she is a micro manager and control freak. Even trying to come up with an example is hard for me because I can't remember any of them; that's what can happen when something is of low importance! The very best response for a leader to give when someone asks them to make a decision of low importance is to encourage them to make the decision.

2. Decisions where you want additional input from leaders before you make a decision of some importance.

A leader needs to be clear on how to say "I have to make a decision and I would like some opinions." Clarity is the key because people can misinterpret the request and think you are asking them to make the decision for you. I've had times where I asked for someone's opinion, heard it, decided to go a different way and then heard them say, "Why did he ask me for my opinion if he didn't take it?" It works best when you clarify that you are seeking different opinions from people so you can process the data before making a decision.

A good example is when a CEO is involved in a sales relationship and needs to make the proposal. The CEO needs input in order to create the best value for the customer and may end up with a half dozen solid ideas. But ultimately, the CEO must make the decision in order to lead the effort.

3. Decisions where consensus is desired because it affects the entire enterprise.

There are decisions that affect the life and direction of the company, and a leader wants collaboration and consensus from the group because there has to be complete ownership by the other leaders for it to work. When we came up with our Vision, Mission and Value statements, every word was debated, and we ended up with complete consensus on the part of the leadership team.

Business is not a democracy, and not all decisions are made by majority rule. Sometimes I bring the entire team into the collaboration, and other times it is a smaller group. When it came to our banking relationship, my CFO and COO were a part of the collaboration, so the three of us had consensus but the CFO had to own that relationship.

It is these types of decisions when the leader should rarely shortcut the conversation and pull the trigger. If the team doesn't own it, you reduce your chances of maximizing your success.

At one point, I had come to the conclusion that we needed to centralize our warranty department and have full time equivalents or FTEs processing the claims. They would become experts, improve the relationship with our supply partner and know the ins and outs in order to maximize what the company was entitled to. Randy, who was in charge of warranty, didn't agree. So I waited for over a year until he finally said, "Let's do it." We did it, and it was the right decision. I could have forced it earlier, and Randy would have complied, but in his gut, he would not have owned it. Because I waited for the right time, Randy owned it and made the most of the change. Today our warranty department is a well-oiled machine, and our recovery rate is one of the better ones in our industry.

4. Important decisions where you go against the group.

The only times you short cut the collaboration process is when there is a time constraint, and you feel it could significantly damage the company or your gut is telling you to go against the common opinion. These circumstances do exist but not often—probably once every five years.

It actually took some reflection and input from the leaders for me to come up with one example, and it's about our last big restructuring. Since rentals are by far our most profitable division, I wanted one member of the leadership group to wake up every day focusing on rentals and driving that focus throughout the company. The team truly felt that each of the leaders could do a satisfactory job with rental in their territory and that such a position was not needed. I made the call and asked Bill to drive the rental business through each of our regions. After one year, we increased our profit in rental by 30 percent. It was the right call. Remember, though, if you make these calls, you have to be right.

Having a diversified leadership team is easy to say and tougher to do. The old adage "birds of a feather flock together" is very true in life and in business. At MH Equipment, we do not have a litmus test for employees or leaders. We don't ask about religious beliefs or political beliefs or thoughts on social justice. Our team is primarily a little to the right of center politically and a little bit left of center in caring for those in need (we give 10 percent of our net income to improve our communities). Where we may disagree with others who are on the left of center on the topic of social programs, we believe it is the individual, churches, synagogues, mosques and not-for-profit mercy ministries that should lead this effort and not the federal government. Both sides agree we need to give a hand up to people that want and need a hand. We just feel the private sector has a passion for it, while the federal government can get caught up in bureaucracy, self-interest and red tape.

There are various areas where we have healthy differences: some are cautious, others are aggressive; some are objective thinkers, others are subjective thinkers; some spend money easily, others are very thoughtful before spending (like Brad, our CFO, which is a good thing); some are strategic, others are more tactical.

We can all have differences, but most importantly we have leaders that fully embrace the Vision, Mission and Values.

Strong, independent, driven leaders that embrace the culture and values of the company may cause personal frustration from time to time but are worth their weight in gold.

CHAPTER 13

VALUES AND CULTURE ARE
THE SECRET SAUCE

When you're committed to your company values, your actions may surprise other people.

At one point, our primary supply partner, Hyster Yale Group, paid for MH to have a strategic planning session with GE/Wells Fargo facilitators. The lead facilitator was a woman named Mary who had been in the business for 40 years. At the end of the three-day session, we came up with a four-year strategy to increase our sales by 100 percent. We knew that it would require organic growth, acquisitions and additional revenue channels. At the end of the retreat, Mary asked me in front of the group, "John, are you fully committed to our strategic plan?"

I responded, "Absolutely...not."

Needless to say, Mary was somewhat shocked, three days into a meeting with 15 of us, to hear the boss throw a wet blanket on the proceedings.

I said, "I will not do anything to achieve a goal that goes against our value statements. So we will try to achieve the plan but not at the expense of our values." Then I added, "When you chase numbers, you make bad decisions."

This could possibly be worthy of repeating: "WHEN A COMPANY CHASES NUMBERS, IT MAKES BAD DECISIONS." It's equally true in both business and personal life.

Mary ended our time together by announcing, "In my

40 years of working with major corporations, military arms of our government and not-for-profits, I have never seen a company whose written value statements are so closely aligned to reality." Our team felt pretty good about the observation.

I have been in the business world since 1980, and the idea of Mission, Vision and Values can still be confusing. To do a brief overview of these…

Mission

A mission is a statement of the reason for the existence of the organization, the ultimate purpose the organization serves in society and the boundaries within which it operates.

Vision

If the mission describes your reason for being, then the vision describes what you want to become or how you want to be regarded.

Values

Values include beliefs and attitudes that guide behavior and relationships with others.

A simpler way to describe them is:

Mission provides the what: **What** are we doing?

Vision gives an organization direction: **Where** do we want to go?

Values provide the culture: **How** are we going to conduct ourselves?

Peter Drucker said, "Culture will eat strategy for breakfast every day." If MH Equipment has any secret sauce, it is our culture—how we try to conduct ourselves.

Culture is created through our Mission, Vision and Values but primarily through Values. The Vision and Mission at MH Equipment isn't a classic definition because it still includes content of how we want to behave.

Our Vision...
is to be regarded as an employer of choice, a trustworthy partner, and an ethical market leader in our communities by providing our customers innovative solutions and unparalleled value.

Our Mission...
is to deliver exceptional service while honoring our vision and recognizing that:
All people matter and are due honor and respect.
Principled passion inspires others and enriches lives.
Our purpose unites us in serving our customers and community.

A mission can change and sometimes it is necessary to change the mission because the needs of the market can change. And if the mission changes, the vision can also change.

But values are constant—they don't change from year to year. They are also passionate, elicit strong emotion and contain core beliefs or convictions you hold true. They are rudders that drive an organization or person.

Values reflect who we are as people and as a company. More than anything else, our company is driven by our written values and we have one for each of our stakeholders: our Employees, Company, Suppliers, Customers and Communities.

Values are the filters people or companies use to make decisions, and there are two types of value statements: what's written on a wall and then what actually happens within the organization. If the leaders cannot quote and explain the written value statements of a company, I doubt they are the true value statements. We have borrowed a process learned from Horst Schulze's book *Excellence Wins*. Every time our executive team meets, one member reviews our Mission, Vision and Values and talks about how one area of the MVV has recently played out in his life.

Let's look at the value statement for each of our stakeholders and how the values drive our decisions:

Employees

Equipping our Employees is all about providing a safe and encouraging environment that recognizes integrity, inspires passion and enables personal growth.

When we think about our employees, the questions we

ask come from the value statement. Our list is a little atypi-cal: we did not include things simply inherent to a job, like the right tools, equipment, uniforms for technicians or training. We just assume most companies provide the tools necessary to get the job done with quality and efficiency.

This is the list that drives our culture:

We will equip our employees with a safe environment. Physical safety in the service industry is a big deal.

Our technicians work on equipment that weighs up to 100,000 pounds. If I have a bad day in my job, my biggest danger is a nasty paper cut. For our technicians, their worst day is death, and that possibility exists every day.

MH has a couple of mantras: "Be safe in the moment" and "Grab the moment." It is all about being present when you are working on equipment. Our technicians, before they do any repair job, are encouraged to ask themselves, "What could cause me harm on this repair?" Then, they address that concern before beginning the repair. If an employee decides the repair really requires two people for safety, the technicians don't begin until there are two of them.

With any injury or near-miss injury reported, we have a conference call with the employee, their boss, the safety manager, the COO, the regional president and the CEO. We don't do it to assign blame but to seek understanding and attempt to find out what happened and what the company and technician can do to prevent it from ever happening again. Once the call is over, we send a bulletin to all the technicians about what happened and the steps we're taking to make sure it does not happen again.

For the benefit of our office employees, we decided to increase physical security and have secure access at all of our facilities. This expense certainly did not bring in more income, but when we thought about what "safe" meant, we decided that taking steps to protect our employees from random acts of violence aligned with our value statement.

Physical safety isn't the only important part of the value; mental and emotional safety are equally important since mental and emotional abuse can be much more destructive than physical abuse. We will not tolerate any form of discrimination or harassment. Many years ago a long-term employee told a newer employee who was a person of color that if he did something again, he would take him out and lynch him. The guy who said it had worked for the company for over 20 years. Even though he had 20 years' seniority, We said two things to him. The first was a question: "What in the world were you thinking?" The second was a statement: "You are fired."

Our diversity policy does not require our employees to embrace and celebrate all forms of diversity. We have no interest in telling our employees how to think. It is wrong to tell people what they *must* celebrate, especially something against their beliefs. Our diversity policy states, "Our employees will treat all people, regardless of their diversity, with respect and dignity." With over 900 employees, we have a lot of diversity, including several female employees who are in same-sex marriages. If you asked them what I think about same-sex marriage, their response would probably be, "I doubt if he embraces this lifestyle, but I love MH Equipment because I am treated with respect and dignity. And if I was harassed by anyone, I know John would aggressively defend me." We can have different opinions and different takes on life without hating each other.

When it comes to creating an environment that enables personal growth, there is only one person who can change John Doe and that is John Doe. So we strive to create an environment where if John Doe wants to make positive changes, there are support mechanisms to assist.

We desperately want our employees to get on top of their finances, and so we work with the Dave Ramsey organization with a product called "Smart Dollar." It has been an effective tool for those who want to make a change.

We also offer something called "Naturally Slim" for those trying to get their weight under control. It's more an educational program than a diet program, and it's proven to be beneficial for employees working to improve their health.

But perhaps no factor influences an employee's job performance more than his or her home life. Marriage is not for the faint of heart, and when there is a lot of strife at home, it affects the whole person. That's why we pay for the registration and hotel for any of our employees and their significant other to attend something called the Family Life Marriage Conference. It's a conference based on biblical principles—something we communicate clearly to our employees, along with the message that they don't need to be married to attend (we've had employees attend who are single). Over 500 couples within our organization have taken advantage of the offer. This is the letter we send each year.

To: **All MH Employees**
From: John Wieland
Subject: **Family Life Marriage Getaway - "A Weekend to Remember"**

As an employer, it is challenging to find ways to positively influence our employees and families outside of the workplace. The Family Life Marriage Getaway is one of those opportunities. MH Equipment has promoted this seminar for its employees for a number of years and has always received very positive feedback from those who have attended.

The Family Life Marriage Getaway is a non-denominational Christian-based approach to a successful and satisfying marriage. My wife and I attended the conference many years ago and have benefited from the experience and support. We want to make it available to all employees.

This conference can help save or improve a struggling marriage, make a good marriage better or make a great marriage fantastic. It is a strategic opportunity to spend a weekend building something vitally important to each partner. Even if you do not share the Christian faith, this seminar offers many common sense and timeless principles for improving your marriage.

MH Equipment will support your attendance to this seminar by paying for the <u>*registration fees*</u> *and the cost of your* <u>*conference*</u> <u>*hotel*</u> *for two nights. Spouses or significant others are included. If you have attended a conference before, you may attend again.*

One of the most rewarding moments of our doing this is at least once a year we get a letter from an employee or a spouse that goes something like this:

Dear John,

Thank you for the opportunity to go to the Family Life Marriage Conference. My marriage was on the brink and my faith had grown cold. This weekend was a turning point. My wife and I have agreed on a path forward and we both have renewed hope and I have returned to the faith I once had. Thank you.

I tell people that when I get a letter like that, I sit back in my seat and say, "I don't suck as a boss today." It is these letters that motivate me to continue to invest in our employees' marriages.

We also try to help the people we work with who are

outside of MH. When we were doing a lot of rental business with a company in Danville and our main contact was getting a divorce, our salesperson there, Jim Skinner, asked if we would pay to send our contact to the Family Life Marriage Conference. I said, "Great idea!" The guy reluctantly agreed to attend but afterward ended up rededicating his life to Christ and reaffirming his marriage to his wife. A footnote: he ended up quitting the company because he needed to break with his past path, which included an affair with a coworker. Once he left, we lost all the rental business—almost $250k a year—but he and his wife are still married, and the family unit is intact. Somehow things work out. We recovered and do quite well in Danville, and we would do the exact same thing again because people and families matter.

We want our employees to find purpose outside themselves, so we also give them the opportunity to have eight hours of paid time off to serve at any not-for-profit. This gives them the opportunity annually to perhaps find a passion outside themselves.

Customers

Serving our Customers is accomplished by being consultative in nature, transparent in practice and passionate for being a good steward of their resources.

Those are three big goals. Let's look at them one by one:

Consultative in Nature

This is vastly oversimplifying, but selling is having a certain product and trying to convince a customer to buy it, while consulting is going to your customer with nothing but good knowledge about their business and a lot of questions.

One time, we had a potential customer in Indianapolis who sent out a request for 60 forklift trucks. One thing MH does exceptionally well is being late to the party, and this was no exception. I believe all of our competitors had talked to this customer and quoted the trucks. I also believe the customer agreed to see us simply as a courtesy.

When we got up to the plate, we started to ask a lot of questions and most of them had little to do with the specifications of the forklift trucks. The questions were things like, "Where are you spending money that you feel is out of control?" and "What hurts your operations?"

For this customer, all pain actually centered around his rental spend, which was out of control. We presented a plan that would reduce his company's rental spend by 25 percent in the first six months. He believed us, we took over the rentals and they reduced their rental spend by 25 percent in the first six months. And oh yes, they also gave us the order for 60 trucks.

Transparent in Practice

Many times when I meet with potential customers, at some point in the meeting, I say, "If you choose to do business with us, there is one thing I can promise. We will make mistakes. I also promise we will not try to hide those mistakes. We will let you know what happened, make it right and then communicate how we will avoid this mistake in the future." We want our customers to know they do not have to worry about what we are doing when their backs are turned.

Once when we sold a large lift truck to a customer, everything worked well, but when we put together the leasing document, we received $10,000 too much. We realized we'd made an error, and the customer would never know it. The payments were already set up for the next 60 months. Our salesperson brought this to my attention and asked me what we should do.

Because of the values of the company, it was a pretty easy decision: I asked our contact to lunch, where I told him what had happened, apologized for the mistake, explained what we were doing to keep it from happening again and gave him a check to his company for $10,000. (Yes, he still had me pick up the bill for lunch!)

One of the defining questions we have within the company is this: "If this customer, fellow employee or vendor knew everything about this subject that I do, would we or they still say they were treated fairly?"

Passionate about Being a Good Steward of Their Resources

If there is one word that weaves its way through my business and life, it's "stewardship." A good definition of it is: *The careful and responsible management of something or someone entrusted to one's care.*

At one point, we had a great company that was renting over 100 trucks from one of our branches. Now, every dollar of revenue is not equal, and our most profitable dollar by far is the rental dollar, followed by service, parts and equipment sales.

This relationship was very profitable for MH, but we were not being a good steward of our customer's resources. There are reasons from time to time for a company not to do a long-term lease or buy equipment— perhaps because they do not have the money to spend on capital expenditures or because they want to keep these assets off their balance sheet.

We talked to our customer continuously about approaching the program differently. After a year and a half of encouraging the customer to make a different choice, he finally pulled the trigger and entered into a long-term lease agreement. This was truly the best use of his company's resources; it reduced their spend by over $250,000 a year. But it also reduced our profits by over $250,000, which was more than half of the profit for the branch.

Why would we keep pushing to do something that would have such a negative impact on our branch? Because it was in the best interest of our customer. Yes, we made a lot less money at the branch, but we have also kept this customer ever since. If we hung on for the cash cow, another provider would have showed them a better way and been the hero, while we would have been on the outside looking in.

When customers truly believe that you are consultative, transparent and a good steward of their resources, business can be a lot of fun. You can become partners and friends.

Once, when we were working with a Fortune 100 company on a national contract, they requested references. Every customer asks for references, but not all of them mean it; this company meant it. A group of eight people interviewed three Fortune 100 customers of ours for two hours apiece. After that, the company made the decision to partner with us, primarily because of what our other customers said about doing life with MH.

I've told our executive team we want to be the Pete Rose of business (without the lingering gambling problem question!). We want to make a reasonable profit over a long period. We are not swinging for the fences; a single, a walk or a hit by pitch is good for us!

Company

Strengthening our Company is accomplished by disciplined effort to pursue effective relationships and implement sound business practices ensuring the long-term well-being of the company and employees.

Bow to the Enterprise

Our leadership group espouses the phrase, "From a

secular standpoint, we bow to the enterprise." To be clear, we are not suggesting that we bow to an enterprise instead of God, which is why we say "from a secular standpoint." The word "bow" means loyalty and submission, and there is nothing more important than what and who you bow to. When it comes to the advancement of an individual or the sustainability of the enterprise, the enterprise has to take the highest priority.

When Julie and I purchased MH Equipment in 1994, we didn't know if we would be in business two years later. At the time, I had one overarching goal: DO NOT GO BANKRUPT. Many people have filed for bankruptcy and still became very successful. But I do have a pride issue: if I filed for bankruptcy, I would feel like I had a big "Loser" sign on my forehead forever. Today, I have one overarching goal for my company: DO NOT GO BANKRUPT. While the leadership team of MH has worked hard to have a strong company and balance sheet, I know things can change very quickly.

One of the benefits of being a privately held company is you never have to chase numbers for a month or a quarter or a year just to make analysts happy. Every decision we make is viewed with long-term vision.

Publicly traded companies will be conflicted. Do they do something to make one quarter look better even if it isn't a good decision in the long term, or do they accept having a bad quarter knowing the direction they are going is better for them in the long run?

We have communicated to our employees that the most important stakeholder is not the employees, as most people would think, but the company. If we are not healthy as a company, our ability to live out our values with our other stakeholders would become very difficult.

If we have a healthy company, consider what we can do with the other stakeholders:

Employees

- We don't have layoffs during the Covid 19 pandemic;
- We can spend money on safety and secured access;
- We can train our employees;
- We can give merit increases or bonuses;
- We can aggressively match the 401k;
- We can invest in improving benefits;
- We can have Wellness, Healthy Choices, Naturally Slim, Smart Dollar and Marriage Conferences;
- We can attract and retain good employees.

Customers

- We can have sufficient inventory for good response time;
- We can make concessions for the sake of a long-term relationship;
- We can be good stewards of our money in accordance with our value statement;

- We can aggressively pursue new customers even when it may not be profitable in the beginning.

Suppliers

- We pay our bills on time;
- We carry sufficient inventory to represent their product;
- We can have give and take, like any relationship requires;
- We can have long-term partnerships with suppliers, since they want to grow with healthy companies.

Communities

- We can provide charity time off;
- We can be good corporate citizens;
- We can have food drives and Operation Christmas Child;
- We can have a foundation to come alongside our passions.

If you bow to the long-term health of the enterprise, you will have options, and in 2020, options were needed.

Perhaps there's no better example of how quickly things can change than the impact of the coronavirus.

My friend who owns a bus company had strong revenue but when coronavirus hit, he had to lay off 90 percent of his staff in a week. Hospitality, entertainment, airlines and restaurants went from "life is great" to "life is a disaster" in almost the blink of an eye. I have no idea how I would have handled being in charge of a company in one of those industries.

Our industry actually fared better than some. We were fortunate to be considered an essential business, which meant that we could still go to work as long as we made various accommodations. Having a strong balance sheet helped us weather the storm. And in 2020, there was a lot of rain!

Our business did slow down a fair amount, especially during April, May and June of 2020, but the executive team unanimously agreed that we would not have any layoffs during this time. Our logic was that our employees had worked hard over the previous few years to build a strong company, so it made perfect sense for us to invest back some of our profits into the employees that helped create the profits in the first place. While we knew that doing this could actually create a loss for the year, we were committed to our plan. It also gave us an opportunity to live out our Vision as an Employer of Choice and our Value that People Matter.

The way we kept our technicians and other people employed was by having them work at a not-for-profit organization, serving our communities or doing acts of kindness while still being paid and receiving benefits. During those three months, we provided our communities with over 11,000 hours of charity time.

Normally at that time of year, we have a company-wide initiative for food pantries called Battle of the Branches where we gather food items and distribute them locally in the communities we serve. Food pantries were of course in bad shape at that time: their food supply was drying up, and what they needed more than anything was funding to strategically purchase food to meet their clients' needs. And so we decided to not do the normal Battle of the Branches and instead changed the name to "Purpose Unites." Rather than collecting food, we asked our employees to consider giving financially through payroll deduction for six pay periods, with the Foundation tripling their gift. This meant that if an employee gave $10 per paycheck, we would turn it into $30. Each branch got to decide where in their community their money went. In those four days of the campaign, we raised $180,000 for our local food banks.

Life always seems to go a little bit better during the tough patches when you turn your eyes towards those in need and then invest in their journey.

Amazingly, with the slowdown in the economy, keeping all our employees fully employed, providing our communities with over 11,000 hours of charity, raising over $180,000 for our food banks and not receiving any funds from the United States government, we had our most profitable year ever. The year 2020 will be remembered for many to come and, overall, it will be remembered as a dark time. For MH Equipment, it was our finest hour.

Worldview Meets Business Head-on

With the craziness of the federal government giving

away programs during the coronavirus crisis, it appeared there was a path for MH to receive funds. Hyster Yale Group applied for a franchise code for their dealers. If they received it, dealers with over 500 employees could apply based on regions. MH was told that the franchise code was forthcoming, so we were working with a bank to get ready to process the application. The four-division request totaled over $12 million—a fair amount of money. But there was a catch: in order to process the application, the bank needed us to answer "NO" to a question on the application that was truthfully a "YES."

*Question 3 - Is the Applicant or any owner of the Applicant an owner of any other business, or have common management with, any other business? If yes, list all such businesses and describe the relationship on a separate sheet identified as addendum A.**

I understood that they were asking this to make sure we did not have over 500 employees with common owner-ship. And our four divisions not only had common owner-ship but the exact same ownership.

I asked the representative from the bank how I could answer yes. She said, "If you say 'NO,' we will assume you are telling the truth and submit it. The SBA would have to go through the vetting, and if it turned out you were not telling the truth, you could have to pay it back."

When all the information was provided, Hyster Yale didn't get the code we as a dealer needed, and there were other hurdles which caused us to be ineligible. So we were dead in the water from the start. But for one day I really thought if we marked "NO," we were going to get over $12 million.

But I remembered the story of Abraham and Isaac where God told Abraham to go and sacrifice his one and only son. God had no intention of having Abraham kill his son, but he wanted to test Abraham. Abraham didn't know it was a test and was willing to obey God because God had promised descendants through Isaac, so he had faith God would somehow save him.

I felt I was in a similar position—that God already knew the outcome—but I was being tested. Would I check the box for $12 million? I told the bank if falsifying the document was the only way, we would have to walk away from the opportunity.

This is a small example of how your worldview and business have to fit hand in glove. If I would have checked "YES" and then received the money or not received the money, I would always know money was my god and not God.

An interesting postscript to this story: I was bragging about my piety to my 22-year-old son and he responded, "Before you give yourself the Mother Teresa of the Year Award, remember that it wasn't overly difficult for you; you already have enough. What would you have done if your company was about to go bankrupt?" I hate that kid! (Do I get to claim credit for how wise my kid is for correcting me?)

He had a great point. It's my deepest hope to stay true to my conviction, but I shouldn't act high and mighty saying "no" to something that wasn't even close to life or death for me.

Suppliers

Partnering with our suppliers is accomplished through affiliation with highly respected manufacturers to represent their products with diligence and professionalism.

As I've explained, MH's primary partner is Hyster Yale Group, the original equipment manufacturer of forklift trucks. The longer I'm in the business, the more I understand the importance of this relationship.

It truly is a partnership: each side has a responsibility.

First, Hyster/Yale, as a highly respected manufacturer in business for over 75 years, must make a quality product. It's one of the largest manufacturers of lift trucks in the world and boasts the largest range of types and capacities in the industry. Having a large range is important but not as important as making a quality product. When there is quality product coming out of the factories and the reputation is strong in the industries, the sales process is much easier.

But on the flip side, MH needs to represent Hyster/Yale's products with diligence and professionalism. MH has done a great job fulfilling this with our supply partners...at times! There have been other times when we have completely swung and missed.

One reason we've maintained a healthy relationship with HYG is that we refuse to keep score. In any relationship, there are going to be times when you think you didn't get a fair shake on an issue and vice versa. What happens many times in business with supply partners when something doesn't go your way is that you think, "Okay, but I will remember this" and when you get them back, you get them a little more than they got you. This is a downward spiral leading to a very negative place.

We have challenged ourselves to fight the good fight on issues we think are just, but then, after the issue has been resolved, good or bad, we move on. There is really no other option if you want to have a healthy relationship.

MH is considered one of the more successful HYG dealers in the nation, but we are sure not perfect or even the best. One phrase we like in our company is "Stay humble, stay hungry, don't settle." When some companies achieve a certain status, they start to lose the "stay humble" part. We are pretty sure all wisdom does not reside within the executive committee of MH. If HYG challenges us in areas where we are not performing, we take that information seriously. Is there a reason we need to be one of the best in this area and, if so, what do we need to do to achieve success?

HYG sees what makes a good dealer in a specific area. When they raise their hand on a performance issue, we tend to believe it is for our benefit, too. One time they told us we were doing a terrible job at the end of lease decisions for customers who lease trucks from us. After internal discussions, we decided that it wasn't only a case of not being smart financially, but also not serving our customers as well as we could. So we hired someone to manage the end-of-lease decisions. In a matter of months, we went from being one of the worst performers to the top performer in this area. We ended up serving our customers better, and it improved our overall financial position.

We started to consider ourselves the kings of end-of-lease activity with our customers—that is, until HYG told us that we were one of the worst dealers when it came to getting the paperwork in after a customer returned the lease. If the paperwork isn't done in a timely manner, our customer would get another invoice after returning the truck. Although the invoice would ultimately be credited, it was a major inconvenience for the customer. So we reviewed our process, asked one employee to manage it and virtually eliminated the issue of paperwork not getting to the appropriate destination. This in turn helped our customer avoid an extra headache.

The point is if a partnership is worth having, it is worth investing sufficient resources to make sure you are doing your part. If both sides aren't winning, it will create unnecessary tension. The Original Equipment Manufacturer understands strong, stable dealers will sell more of their product in the long run. And dealers understand if their OEM partner is profitable and invests in research and development, they will have better products to sell.

At one point, we also carried construction equipment manufactured by a company called JCB in four of our branches. JCB has a great market share in Europe but not so much in America and especially not in the Midwest, where Cat and John Deere are competitors. We were not moving the needle for JCB in those markets very well and decided to focus only on one market: Indianapolis. We mutually agreed to vacate Cincinnati, Louisville and Charleston. Over the next few years, our numbers were improving, but as we thought about our value statement of "representing their product with professionalism and diligence," no one in the executive committee could say we were embracing this value. So we fired ourselves, telling JCB we were not embracing our value statement and weren't willing to make the investments to achieve our values. JCB wasn't exactly happy about our decision but respected our desire to fully live out our values.

Communities

Investing in our communities produces a positive impact by coming alongside our employees' passions with support and financial assistance through our "His First Foundation" charitable program.

His First Foundation

In July of 2001, we had just lost $700,000. Hyster was going to give us $300,000 in incentives, and the leadership group felt we could make up the rest by the end of the year. I was actually leading—finally.

The executive team met in my basement to talk about our value statements. We had said we wanted to make a difference in our communities, but up to that point we were doing what a lot of companies do: giving $100 here, $500 there and an occasional $1,000 someplace else. We agreed that we were not making a significant impact on any community.

Julie and I have seen the beauty and joy of giving to others since we were married—not reluctantly or under compulsion but cheerfully. I always felt that when I take money out of the company for reasons other than to pay taxes, I would do my tithes and offerings. But there was a problem: from 1994 to 2001, I had not taken a single penny out of the company other than to pay taxes. That didn't feel good to Julie or me. I had read a book by Larry Burkett called *Business by the Book*—a great book if you want to be convicted like all get out. In fact, outside of the business principles that come from the Bible, this book has had the biggest impact on my business approach.

I told the group I wanted to start a foundation called His First Foundation and commit 10 percent of our net income—budget or actual, whichever was greater—to it. We had complete support and a start date of January 2002. There was one problem: I wanted to start immediately, in July of 2001, right after we'd lost $700,000. You could understand the hesitancy on the part of the team. The compromise we made was I would guarantee the dona-tion: if we did not make the budget and still gave 10 percent of the budgeted income to the foundation, I would personally make up the deficit.

We did make the budget, and with the incentives from

Hyster, we ended up losing $90,181 for the year. And the foundation was off and running.

The design of the foundation is to align itself with our employees' passions and celebrate with them.

1. We support "non-denominational" faith-based organizations whose mission is to share the love of Jesus Christ or meet the physical needs of people in His Name.

I am not ashamed of the Gospel; a community is better off when they have a thriving faith community ministering to others. For the most part, we stay away from supporting the local church; I wanted to avoid criticism from people that would say the foundation was created to support my local church. But we will support any service ministries, such as the Salvation Army or Samaritan's Purse, and we will support missionary trips and missionaries.

2. We support secular good works organizations.

We know we have plenty of employees who do not embrace Christ, and we want to support their passions as well. There are tremendous secular organizations serving our communities with excellence and compassion.

I mentioned our annual "Battle of the Branches" event where each branch collects food and funds and then decides which food pantry or food bank will receive the donations, but we also have standard donations for local youth programs, especially those that include the children of our employees. The fact that we've determined a set amount to donate has saved a lot of frustration and disappointment over the years. Regardless of your role in the company, there is no variation on the level of support.

There are no limits to what we will support as long as it makes a community better. We have supported chess clubs, karate clubs and boxcar derbies. My passions may not be someone else's passions, and someone else's passions may not be my passions—that's what makes the world go around. We believe when people find a passion outside of themselves, it is a game changer. Life is awfully difficult when it centers around you. When someone has a passion outside themselves, their life becomes more balanced. They actually end up being a more balanced person in general and actually become a more reliable employee.

3. We support simple "acts of kindness."

Several years ago in Bowling Green, Kentucky, a young man in the community was involved in an accident and became paralyzed from the waist down. We have a branch there, and our team wanted to retrofit his house with ramps. They asked the foundation for $5,000 for the hardware, with the idea that we would also provide technicians and office people for the labor. The branch manager talked to the parents of the boy, and they were shocked that a group of people from a company they knew nothing about would do this for their family.

The date of the big retrofit was set. The local news got wind of it and came to the house during construction. The reporter asked our branch manager, "How do you know the young man?"

"We don't," the branch manager responded.

The reporter went to the second reason why we would do something like this. "Do his parents work for a good customer of yours?" he asked.

Again, the response was, "We don't know his parents or where they work."

Now the reporter was perplexed. Her final question was, "Why, then, are you doing it?"

Our branch manager simply responded, "We believe all people matter."

Similarly, in November of 2013, an EF4 tornado in Washington, Illinois caused losses of close to a billion dollars. It destroyed over 500 houses. Not damaged, but destroyed. Actually, at one house the second story window drapes were still on the rod on the inside, but the lower half of the drapery was on the outside of the house. The window was closed, so how did that happen? The tornado lifted the roof, the drapery and the outside of the house, and then the roof came back down. In the same house, in the bathroom adjoining the bedroom with the drapery, there was a Kleenex box on the back of the toilet that didn't move.

We decided to do something unique. Most social agencies provide resources to the homeless or people in need and tell them exactly how they can spend it: "Here is a gift card to buy gas for your car" or "Here is a certificate to buy clothes" or "Here is a certificate to buy groceries."

We decided we were going to give each family who lost their home a $500 Visa card with absolutely no parameters. We used the Salvation Army to facilitate the program, and it was a struggle for them to accept the fact that we would not know how the money was to be used. But we felt that these families had gone through something nobody wanted to go through, and if they wanted to use the Visa to take the family to the movies, great. If they wanted to forget their problems and get drunk, that was their decision.

The night of the town hall meeting was unique. There were close to 1,000 people jammed into an auditorium. The mayor of Washington, Gary Manier, was masterful during this time. He was approachable, worked tirelessly and pursued and received all the federal assistance he could.

Gary asked me to address the crowd and to have a moment of prayer, telling me to say anything I wanted to. I don't know what really happened, but it was a holy moment. You could hear a pin drop. It felt like everyone there realized the Grace they had received during the tornado. There was one death and another died later from complications from an injury. All I remember saying is, "This night is not about the mayor, nor my company, nor the people in the room. This night is about the Mercy and Grace of God on the community of Washington."

The Salvation Army included a pamphlet on how to navigate a crisis and a pamphlet regarding spirituality during this time with each Visa card. In addition to the gift card, our company added a small piece of paper that said:

A Special Note:

Jesus knows suffering all too well. You didn't choose this road but Jesus actually chose the road of suffering to demonstrate His Love and desire for you by taking our sin upon Him at the Cross. May you fully experience the love of Jesus Christ, knowing His Presence and Peace.

Five hundred dollars did not fix anyone's problems. The people in Washington needed dollars, and we gave them a penny. But it gave the community a good night. Sometimes in life that is all you can do—just give someone a good moment.

Final Thoughts

There are many ways to reflect your values, and it was our leadership team's choice to have a specific value statement for each of the five stakeholders of the company.

But there is one thing we didn't do. We did not pay a consulting firm $5,000,000 or $50,000 or $5 to help come up with the values. These are our values and no one else's. In hindsight, for us, this was a good call.

The process took at least six months. We discussed, debated, argued and fought over every single word. Words are important, and we worked on them until we had complete consensus.

We also discovered, by accident, that there is perfect alignment between our value statements. Many companies have competing values or filters, such as "We want to maximize shareholder return" as well as "We want to do what is best for the customer." Most people would realize there is a tension between these two value statements. If a company tries to maximize profit, I promise you they won't be doing what is best for the customer. And if a company is doing what is best for the customer, many times it is not going to be maximizing profits. Values and filters need to be aligned. When you see a lot of dysfunction in a company, you may want to look at competing values. Many times this conflict could be the reason for the dysfunction.

We got lucky. Our company didn't seem to have the same level of dysfunction as others. We found out there were no tensions in our value statement. For example, being a good steward of our customer resources aligns with implementing sound business practices that ensure the long-term well-being of the company and employees. They fit because if a company does what is right for the customer, they will keep the customer for a long time, which ensures the company's long-term health.

Remember, part of our Mission is embracing the fact that all people matter and are due honor and respect. Well, it took a few conversations on an airplane to drive that point home in a series of short stories.

CHAPTER 14

INTERESTING PEOPLE

If you're open to it, you can meet the most interesting people when you fly. It's amazing the types of conversations you can have on an airplane. It is the perfect set up. You sit next to a person who doesn't know you from Adam, and you don't know them from Eve. People who understand this dynamic have no limit to what they will talk about—even the deep dark secrets they have kept private. "Hey, this Joe Blow will never see me again, and it is good for the soul to say some things out loud." If people see someone is really interested in hearing their story, most people take that as a compliment.

I've learned a lot from people that I talk to on a plane.

A Different Lifestyle

One day we were boarding the airplane waiting to get to our seat. The lady boarding in front of me was short, stocky, short haired and had somewhat of a masculine

appearance about her. I know profiling can cause problems, but there was a passing thought that the young lady
may live a different lifestyle than what I am living.

I was on the phone with one of the owners, Bill. We
were talking about spiritual things. I think the topic at
hand that day was King Jesus. I don't know the exact
comments being made, but if you heard my end of the
conversation, you would assume this guy is one of those
"Christian People." I realized the lady standing in front of
me, waiting to get her seat, had caught on to what I was
talking about and who I "was." I felt this freeze come over
our space. It was her worst nightmare to be sitting in the
middle seat of row 23 when I had the aisle seat on row 23.
The hair on her neck stood up when she knew who she
was sitting by. It was clear this lady did not want to sit
next to me.

As a Christian, I have to own this response. Over the
years, this lady has been judged by *Christians*. We have
acted self-righteously. Some Christians have probably told
her she was going straight to hell. Instead of feeling the
true love of Jesus, she has felt the hatred of man. That is
really disappointing, and *we* Christians have to do better.

I made a decision right then and there: in the next two
hours, she was going to leave the plane feeling she had
met at least one Christian who was kind, gracious and
loved like Jesus loved.

Initially this proved difficult. I would ask a question
and she would give me a one-word answer. I would ask
her an open-ended question, and she would close it. She
finally told me she liked to hike with her partner. I think

she had had enough of me and was hoping if she said "partner" I would realize the person I was talking to was a lesbian and go back into my Christian cocoon. I took it as an opportunity to go deeper. I told her I'd just read a book on survival called *Deep Survival — Who Lives, Who Dies, and Why* by Laurence Gonzales about the things people who survive catastrophes have in common. We spent an hour talking about this book and the outdoors. (Pretty amazing, since I've camped in like...never.) I asked her what her name was and she said Sarah. I told her I would love to send her the book if she would give me her address, and she gave me her personal address. Big walls had been broken down in less than two hours. The fact that she went from hating the fact that she was stuck with me to giving me her personal address was beautiful. I sent her the book with a note saying how nice it was to meet her and hear her story. Sarah and I didn't get into spiritual conversations that day, but I do know Sarah did meet a Christian who, for at least two hours, actually reflected the love and beauty of Jesus. For me, that was a good day.

A Different Faith

Another time, I was traveling home from Bentonville, Arkansas after another unsuccessful trip to Walmart trying to convince them they would be more profitable if they did business with me. (If any of you can help a brother out! Just saying!) On the way home I was seated in the back half of the plane and sat by a lady. She was dressed in a style familiar to India. Our flight was to last about an hour and a half, so I decided to say hi. She had a book in her hand, so I asked her what the book was about. Before long she started to share her story.

Her name was Padma Viswanathan. She was a professor of literature at the University of Arkansas, an author and a playwright. Her husband was a poet and they had a son and daughter. Padma was of Indian descent but was born and raised in Canada. Her primary belief system came from Hinduism. I read one of her books, a novel called *The Ever After of Ashwin Rao*. Very interesting book. The premise was how people grieved after the Air India Flight 182 disaster when a passenger jet explosion off the coast of Ireland on June 23, 1985 claimed the lives of all 329 passengers and crew members. Sikh extremists were accused of sabotaging the Air India aircraft.

After we talked about her story, Padma asked me about the book I had with me. I said it was the Bible. As a Hindu, she had some knowledge of Jesus and wanted to know more about why I believed what I believed. Padma asked a lot of questions. For some of the questions I had quick answers. For others, my answer was, "That is a really good question. I don't know the answer to that." I think Padma appreciated the honesty. She was going to look at the Book of John from the Bible in her literature class the next semester and asked if I would be a reference for her as she would receive questions from the class. We did that, and it was fun.

There were some really good and honest questions from her students like the following:

"Was Christ's crucifixion always the plan or did it end up the plan after the Garden of Eden didn't work, the flood didn't work, the Ten Commandments didn't work, Mosaic Law didn't work, etc.?"

That is a very thought-provoking question. I do think it was always the plan based partly on what Peter said in his first letter.

I Peter 1:18:

You know that you were ransomed from the futile ways inherited from your fathers, not with perishable things such as silver or gold, 19 but with the precious blood of Christ, like that of a lamb without blemish or spot. 20 **He was destined before the foundation of the world** *but was made manifest at the end of the times for your sake. 21 Through him you have confidence in God, who raised him from the dead and gave him glory, so that your faith and hope are in God.*

Also, Revelation 13 talks about the names written before the "foundation of the world" in the book of life of the Lamb that was slain.

But her question is still a great question: "Why the garden, why the flood, why the law?" There is no doubt God interacts with man and responds accordingly, so who knows for sure? I'm going to spend some time leaning into that question. Thanks, Padma!

Another question from Padma: "From a Christian perspective, where do people like me, Padma, stand, who know the stories of Jesus but do not consider themselves Christian? People for centuries have wondered, 'Can a Muslim still be a Muslim and embrace Jesus as Lord, can a Hindu hold to their faith and customs and still be saved?'"

This was my response to Padma: there is only one person in the New Testament who was guaranteed eternal life. He was the sinner on the Cross. I'm pretty interested in what his theology was since Jesus said to him, "Today, you will be with Me in paradise." So what was his theology? In short, his theology was:

- I have a problem (a gap between a Righteous God and sinful man).
- Jesus, You are the answer (You can close the gap).
- Please remember me (do close the gap).

Whatever people do with their faith and customs is one thing, but there is one question people at some time will answer. Is Jesus really *the* answer for the gap between me and my Creator? If you say yes and embrace Him as your Savior, you are His child now and forever more, and whatever else you do about different customs is somewhat inconsequential.

Consider reading the New Testament one more time not as a piece of literature but whether it is Truth. Christians believe God desires all people to be saved and come to know the Truth (I Timothy 2:3-4). Jesus Christ did not die for only the Jews. He died and took our punishment upon Him so all people could have an **eternity** with Him.

My final comment to Padma was: "When all is known, I think we will realize you and I sitting next to each other on the plane was not by chance. I know I have grown from meeting you!"

Attractive People

There was a stretch where it seemed I was on an

airplane monthly. One time the person sitting next to me in the middle seat was an unusually attractive woman. She told me her story and how it had been a series of bad choices and how relationships ended up in hurt and pain. I listened intently, empathized with her and told her about this one guy who loves unconditionally, doesn't want anything from her and actually loved her so much, He died for her. His name was Jesus. I left the plane that day feeling I honored God and showed His love to a broken soul.

But as I thought about these conversations with attractive women, I started to think about who I talk to and who I don't, preferring to read a book. I talk to successful-looking people. I talk with athletic-looking people. I talk to attractive people. I find myself reading a book when the one next to me does not fit the above criteria.

This is my confession: I've been taught by my parents and Jesus to care for all people, not just those who look physically attractive, successful or physically strong. But my actions reveal I'm interested in hearing people's stories and sharing my story based on their appearance. What hypocrisy! I say I try to follow Jesus and His Teachings, yet I'm a respecter of people's looks and status.

Lord, help me to see people like You do. You have a special heart for the marginalized of our society. Please change my heart of stone into a heart of flesh so I may share your love with everyone You put into my life.

CHAPTER 15

COUNT THE COST?

Jesus tells a story in the Gospel of Luke:

Suppose one of you wants to build a tower. Won't you first sit down and estimate the cost to see if you have enough money to complete it? For if you lay the foundation and are not able to finish it, everyone who sees it will ridicule you, saying, "This person began to build and wasn't able to finish."

Or suppose a king is about to go to war against another king. Won't he first sit down and consider whether he is able with ten thousand men to oppose the one coming against him with twenty thousand? If he is not able, he will send a delegation while the other is still a long way off and will ask for terms of peace.[1]

There was a company called Oorja Corporation that developed and manufactured direct methanol fuel cell (or DMFC) based power systems that use methanol, combining a fuel cell and traditional battery to provide a high-power solution that significantly reduces operating costs and greenhouse gas emissions. (In case you think I'm really smart, I should tell you that I got that from their website.)

We thought Oorja had a pretty good product and one day, one of our executives was talking to their CEO. They got along well and ended up discussing different types of relationships, including making MH Oorja's master distributor. I'll admit that I kind of liked the term master distributor. When I asked what it meant, our executive told me it meant that we would buy their production and then sell to other distributors and make a ton of money. This was true: if it worked, we would have made millions of dollars. I asked our guy what would happen if this new innovation wasn't embraced by our industry. The answer was we would be stuck with worthless inventory.

"And how much would that be?"

His answer: "About $9,000,000."

Our equity at the time was around $6,000,000, which meant that if we were wrong, it would cost us our company.

A couple of things came to mind. First, we were not going to put our company at risk to help anyone else reach their dreams. Secondly, we will never make a big decision for our company without first counting the costs. If we said yes and the innovation failed, our company would be done. Even if we could make $5,000,000 a year on this agreement, we simply could not risk the company.

We still liked the prospect of this product but we decided to measure our loss and decided once we lost

$150,000 on this venture, we would be done. What happened? Well, if there was an award for quickly and efficiently losing $150,000, I would be giving my acceptance speech. We lost it in a heartbeat, and that was okay. We felt the upside potential was worth risking $150,000, so we were not upset. The industry simply didn't embrace the new technology, so we embraced our parameters and walked away. Nothing ventured, nothing gained.

In hindsight, this was the best $150,000 we have ever lost in the history of our company because if we had decided to go for the gold, MH Equipment would be no more, and the CEO of MH would go down as a rotten CEO who cost hundreds of people their jobs.

When I worked for KPMG, I audited a very stable and sound construction company that purchased a manufacturer of modular homes. It seemed like a reasonable idea, but the economy shifted on them. The company leader didn't understand the business very well and, in a few years, the entire company went into bankruptcy and dissolved.

There are two aspects of acquisitions—the initial purchase price and then potential ongoing losses of the business acquired. When we purchased the dealership in Nebraska and South Dakota, what we paid was fair market value of the assets. No goodwill, no blue sky. I was quite proud of myself on purchasing this dealer. Then, for three years in a row, the newly acquired division lost $300,000. The acquisition turned out to be a very expensive decision.

There have been countless organizations that acquire

companies and communicate to shareholders that the acquisition price was very reasonable. Companies seem to be especially enamored with other companies that have new "intellectual property." But when a company buys another company with "intellectual property," typically no parameters are placed on how much more money will be invested before the new venture is shut down. You can buy a company for $50 million, lose $40 million a year for five years trying to develop the product and by then discover that the cheese has moved, and new technology has made your technology obsolete. The cheap purchase price wasn't so cheap.

The book *Billion Dollar Mistakes* by Steven Weiss focuses on counting the costs before you make any acquisition. In all acquisitions you can expect the following:

1. You don't retain the sales you think you will.
2. The projected synergies are always much greater than actual.
3. Retention of key employees falls short.
4. Conversion of company culture is typically a disaster.

Don't believe you will be the person to avoid these pitfalls. Instead, go in believing you will experience them and be able to survive. I have gone through a dozen or so acquisitions—some small, some substantive. I am pretty sure we've experienced all of these pitfalls to some degree on our acquisitions.

Whether you are entering a different market, pursuing

new technologies or making a hefty acquisition, take the advice of a guy who knew a thing or two about life (that would be Jesus, not me):

Count the Cost

When making decisions, counting the cost is a must and knowing the facts is also essential. Let me tell you a short story on how you can make bad decisions when being too quick to give an opinion.

CHAPTER 16

KNOW ALL THE FACTS

Unfortunately, I have an incredible ability to hear only a small portion of the facts and still be able to develop strong emotional opinions by filling in the missing facts needed to form an opinion.

I have done this for years. You would think with so many years of practice that I would be pretty good at it. And I do believe I'm better than I used to be. When I first started doing this as a young lad, I was probably correct one out of 20 times. Today I am happy to say that I am probably correct one out of 19 times. This means if I lived until I was 200, I would be batting .250, which even people who don't know about baseball understand isn't very good.

My COO, Coit, suffers from the same problem. You would think that since we're the two leaders of the same company, MH Equipment would be completely dysfunctional. And it surely would be but for one saving grace: we both know that we are prone to do these things, so we never make spur of the moment decisions, especially when they involve people.

For some reason, our tendency is to think people say or do things for the worst possible reason. We go straight to the worst-case scenario, and we sit there and stew about it. We complain about these horrible scenarios to each other, and then we admit we are both crazy for thinking that way, laugh about it and say we won't do it anymore. And we don't—until the next time.

There's perhaps no better example of this than when I took my biannual road trip to every branch in 2020, the year of the pandemic. At each branch, I gave my state of the union of our company, hoping to inspire our employees to grow personally. Of course, this was the year 2020. Some people wore masks, some people were careful about social distancing and some people felt safe enough to simply go on with their lives. I traveled over 5,000 miles, giving my presentation 43 times at 31 locations over four weeks. Amazingly, I never got tired of it. With every new audience it felt like a new talk, so I stayed pretty engaged throughout the road trip.

One week I traveled to the Ottawa branch with three people: Woody, who was president of that region; the executive vice president of Employee Services, Angi and Marcie, who was also from Employee Services. When we went into the branch, we did not have masks on or show a lot of awareness about social distancing. The 10 employees from Ottawa, on the other hand, all had face masks on, their chairs were all six to eight feet apart and they wore their masks throughout the entire 50-minute presentation. On our way home that day, we discussed those 10 Ottawa employees. I believe someone in the car (okay, it was me) suggested that wearing masks the whole time was completely unnecessary! I mean, we were in the ware-house with plenty of space and they sat for almost an hour with their masks on. That had to be terribly uncomfortable. Crazy!

The next morning, we went to Danville, Illinois, where there were over 30 people in the training room. There was zero social distancing; people were sitting and standing shoulder to shoulder without masks, and they were sharing donuts and pouring milk out of the same jug. There were many opinions of how to respond to the pandemic. For me, I was not overly concerned about the virus for healthy people and felt that we should have focused more energy on the vulnerable of our society. That's why I told the crew from Danville that I loved them, that they were my favorite branch and they were my kind of people.

When we left Danville and started our trip to Decatur for our next stop, Woody told me he found out what was happening with those employees in Ottawa. He said, "Well, John, the week before your meeting, they had a branch meeting to discuss your visit. They'd heard you'd had a bone marrow transplant a year ago and didn't know if your immune system was at all compromised. So they voted unanimously to wear those stinking masks while you were in the building out of honor and respect for you, *John*!"

Well, that definitely changed some of my opinions. Here's what I've concluded from this experience:

1. Ottawa is now my favorite branch and I love those guys.
2. The guys from Danville evidently could not care less if I lived or died.
3. I need to quit assuming!

While this is a funny story that had few consequences,

how often do we take shortcuts in information gathering while making a decision or forming an opinion and then have it blow up in our face so we suffer meaningful consequences?

Know all the facts!

CHAPTER 17

MONEY

If you want to know the essence of a person, consider their 3 C's:

1. Calendar
2. Conversation
3. Checkbook

A Calendar will tell you where you spend your time. A Checkbook will tell you where you spend your money. Your Conversations will reveal your heart. Let's take these one at a time.

Calendar

We all have 24 hours in a day. Those are precious hours; when an hour is up, it is gone forever, and we don't know how many hours we have left here on this earth. We spend our time in three main ways: work, sleep and discretionary hours. And how you spend your discretionary time reflects who you are. Discretionary time falls into several categories:

1. More work
2. More sleep
3. More personal entertainment
4. More personal care
5. More family time
6. More friend time
7. More time serving others
8. More time seeking spiritual health

The percent of your discretionary time used on each of these will tell a lot about what is truly important to you.

The reason I used "more" in front of the options is that each of these areas are addressed in each of our lives. We all work, sleep and entertain. The challenge we have is managing these options well and determining which may be more important to others. For example:

More work. A lot of men and women get a fair amount of their self-worth from their job or career. Every time they get a paycheck, they are being told they have value, and the bigger the check, the more valuable they are to a company. Some companies like employees to be all in, and I mean *all in*. These people will rise in the food chain at work but often their family life is a complete mess. Most adults want to raise their children to have a strong work ethic; it is a character trait I certainly wish for all my children. We like the idea of someone who starts a job and finishes it. However, when it goes too far, this has a hugely negative effect.

Why do we work? That is the question! The main reason is to support yourself and your family. You have your job to support your family; you do not have your family to support your job. There will be times when you have to make sacrifices. I ask my leadership group periodically, "How much are you stealing from your family?" There may be a season when you are working 50 to 80 hours a week at work, but it cannot be a lifestyle.

All of these options have value to them, and by looking at where people spend their time, will tell you much about what is important to them.

Conversation

What do you laugh about? What do you cry about? Do your conversations tend to always end up on a similar topic? Do you often end up gossiping about others? Do you end up talking about your toys or achievements? Does your humor always end up in the gutter? Do you cry when you see injustice in the world? Reflecting on what your conversations typically look like will again show what is in your mind and in your heart.

Checkbook

The Checkbook is the C that requires the most attention. I highly recommend summarizing your spending on an annual basis, as you will quickly find out where your money is going. A loose translation of what Jesus says is, "Where you spend your money, that is where your heart is." Are you happy with what your spending would reveal about you, or would you be slightly disappointed or embarrassed?

Either way, there are very practical steps you can take to keep you from the poor house.

You need to know how to manage your money effectively, or money problems will follow you until the day you die. Here's what I have shared over the past few years with college seniors who are about to go into the "real" world:

- Avoid accumulation of debt (Prov. 22:7). Julie and I borrowed money when we bought our first house and then paid it off in 10 years. We borrowed some money to build our second home and paid it off in less than 10 years. We bought our cars and appliances with cash, and we even made home improvements with cash. In other words, we try to avoid debt like the plague. There is a proverb that says, "The borrower is the slave to the lender." I've encouraged all of our kids to wait to buy a house until they can borrow only 75 percent so they don't have to get mortgage insurance and also to get a mortgage with an amortization rate of no more than 15 years.

In business, the principles are the same, but the equation is a little different. MH Equipment is in a capital-intensive business, which means we buy a lot of hard assets like forklift trucks for our rental department. It takes a lot of capital to have a big rental fleet, and if done correctly, borrowing money to grow your business is prudent. A simple question to ask in business is, "Are you borrowing the money to grow the business or to meet current payroll?" I think of it like this: you can borrow money to buy a car or borrow money for a tractor. One of them will make you money.

- Never carry a balance on your credit card. I have counseled countless married couples who come to me with financial problems. Every single time, one of them says something like "I owe $30,000 on my credit card." This became such a consistent part of the narrative that I no longer ask people if they have credit card debt. Instead I ask, "How much is your credit card debt?"

When Julie and I got married, we agreed we would never put something on our credit card unless we could pay in full the following month. When we first got married, we needed a washer and dryer. I had a job, Julie had a job, but we also had a higher house payment than we should have had and couldn't afford to pay $600 for a new washer and dryer. We turned our eyes to the want ads and found a small green washer and dryer for $60 total. We could afford $60 and that washer and dryer lasted 10 years at our house. America loves to consume and have immediate gratification: we see something, covet something and then we buy something—even if we can't afford to pay for it. When it comes to debt, there is really no middle ground. You either commit to paying off your credit card monthly or you end up with credit card debt for the rest of your life.

- Manage your debit and ATM cards. When I graduated from college, I got an ATM card that allowed me to go to a machine, put in a card and have money come out. I really liked that! The problem was I never managed it well, so I started to get overdraft notices and would have to pay a $10 fee. While this didn't happen a dozen times, it sure happened more than a few. (Most people are really good with zero and not very good with moderation. If I commit to zero peanut M&M's, I will end up eating zero peanut M&M's. But if I decide to eat them in moderation, I reach into the jar and grab just a few M&M's. I feel good—I didn't take a handful, only a few! Fifteen minutes later, I return to the M&M jar and take out only a few. I am handling this well! It doesn't take a math genius to figure out that by the end of the day, I have been guzzling down M&M's one moderate handful at a time.) And so it was for me with the ATM card: I didn't handle the card well, so I cut it in two and threw it away. I have never had an overdraft from the card again and have been doing just fine without one since 1981.

- Live on one income so you have a choice about whether or not to stay at home with children if you have them. Marriage is not for the faint of heart. Consider my marriage.

These are the extremes of living with Julie.

These are the extremes of living with John.

I wish I could say I was embellishing these lines but they are pretty much spot on. Julie and I have walked through very deep waters in our marriage, and if it was not for God's Grace and Julie's grace, we may not still be married. But we have never had a serious argument about money; that really takes away a lot of pressure. The most common reason for divorce in America is infidelity, but the second most common is money problems. With some basic guidelines, you can avoid the second reason.

Julie and I once taught a young married Sunday school class where we met several times with a young couple who had been married for five years and were going to have their first child. But they had a big problem. With tears in their eyes, they told us that one of them wanted to stay home when they had the baby, but financially, they didn't have that option. My heart bleeds for these couples, but the truth of the matter is they did have a choice; they made it five years earlier when they decided to live on two incomes. They bought a big house, which required a large mortgage, and they bought cars on credit resulting in payments on them. And when it came down to a choice if one could stay home, their past choices made the decision for them.

When Julie and I got married, we decided to live on one income. We knew we could not afford to go into debt, so we lived very modestly. We also knew that having biological children was going to be a challenge, so during the first seven years we were married, we lived on my income and used hers to pay down the principal on the house, save money and support additional ministries. When, in January 1990, we got *the* unexpected call from the doctor where he said he had a new baby girl for us, we did not have nine months to financially plan and prepare. That day, Julie gave notice to her employer, the Department of Children and Family Services, and we went from two incomes to one in the blink of an eye. We also went from a family of two to a family of three. But because of the way we'd been preparing, it was financially seamless.

I make no moral judgment about whether a parent should stay home or work. There's incredible freedom if a couple feels it is in their best interest for both of them to work outside the home. But there are times when a spouse may want to quit work in order to take care of an aging parent or invest in a life passion. Regardless of the reasons, living on one income provides so many more options in life. When both people live on one income, just think of all the options they have.

- Live below your level of income. I love cushion;

life is so much easier when you have it. When your take-home pay and your expenses are equal, you have no cushion, and if your take-home pay is less than your expenses, forget about it. Life like that can be very stressful. Many people allow their standard of living to increase at the same rate or at times at an even greater rate than their standard of earning. You get a raise at your job and then waste no time figuring out how to spend it: a bigger house, bigger cars, a second house, toys and more toys. But really, it's this simple: if you are not producing a cushion, you are producing stress in your life and marriage. Happiness and joy are not dependent on your W-2; there are plenty of incredibly wealthy people who are absolutely miserable. True happiness is when you sleep with your spouse or partner and feel good knowing they are next to you. True happiness is hugging a son or daughter or friend and really meaning it. None of these require money. As my and Julie's earnings increased, our standard of living did not grow very much. The graph below shows directionally how our revenue increased and how our expenses grew.

Lifestyle Pattern

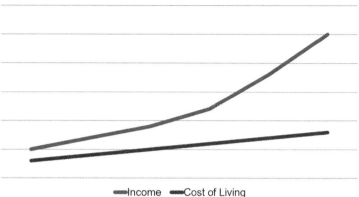

━━ Income   ━━ Cost of Living

- As your salary increases, your rate of giving should increase. There's a funny story I heard about a man who made a covenant with a former pastor to tithe 10 percent of his income every year. He tithed $1000 the year he earned $10,000, $10,000 the year he earned $100,000 and $100,000 the year he earned one million. But the year he earned six million dollars, he just could not bring himself to write out a check for $600,000 to the church. He telephoned the minister, who had long before moved to another church and asked to see him. Walking into the pastor's office, the man begged to be let out of the covenant, saying, "This tithing business has to stop. It was fine when my tithe was $1,000, but I just cannot afford $600,000. You've got to do something, Reverend!" The pastor knelt on the floor and prayed silently for a long time.

Eventually the man said, "What are you doing?
Are you praying God will let me out of the
covenant to tithe?" "No," said the minister. "I am
praying for God to reduce your income back to
the level where $1000 will be your tithe!"

Whether you have spiritual convictions to give money
to the church, organizations or people in need, or you feel
you should give because of your love for humanity, the
goal is to keep giving. I have seen this dozens of times in
my life. People who are charitable always seem to have
less stress in their lives. Whether it is God's Blessings or
luck, there seems to be a connection.

When Julie and I got married, we believed we should
give 10 percent of our gross income to charities. We believe
everything belongs to God, and so it makes sense to show
what we believe by giving money to share the Gospel or to
meet people's physical needs in His name or to a variety of
other places. When we started to make more money, we
began to feel not good about the 10 percent. We asked,
"Why should we be keeping all of this money?" So we
started to increase the percentage—11 percent, 13 percent,
15 percent, 20 percent, and so on. Actually for the last few
years, as we look at our checkbook, our giving has
exceeded our standard of living. Directionally, this is the
total of our earnings, expenses and giving.

Lifestyle Pattern

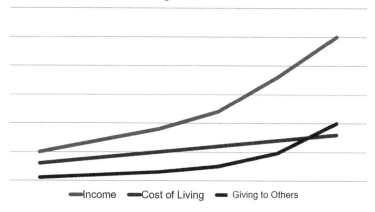

Income   Cost of Living   Giving to Others

- Be in a position to not be a financial burden in your older age.

I always said my dad and mom were asset rich, cash poor, and one of the greatest joys in my life was to be able to provide additional financial security for them. They would have been fine without the help, but it definitely eased their stress, and my siblings truly appreciated it; no one wants to see their aging parents worry about finances. It is also true we don't know what tomorrow will bring, and things outside our control could drastically impact someone's financial stability.

You can save in a way that will provide choices when you are no longer working. At MH we match 50 percent on the dollar up to 10 percent of the employee's income through the 401(k) plan. If they defer 10 percent, we put in five percent for a total of 15 percent. If young people would commit to the idea of contributing to a 401(k), chances are there would not be financial stress when they retire. Our employees in their 60s defer the most, and when I ask younger employees if they think that the older ones wished they would have deferred a higher percent when they were younger, they always say yes. And yet, in general, the younger employees do not contribute aggressively into their retirement. I just don't understand the thinking.

My daughter Jamie graduated from Eureka College, the alma mater of President Ronald Reagan. After graduation, she was looking for a job in Human Resources, and MH had an entry-level position open in the Human Resources department. Jamie knows I had told my children not to come looking to me for a job when they get out of college—I love them too much to do that to them. When children go straight into a business owned by their parents, they will always wonder if they had the right stuff to make it. They need to know they can get jobs on their own.

But Jamie came to me and said, "Dad, it is easier to get a job when you have a job." I can't argue with that logic. She added, "I will still be looking for a position if you give me this job."

I talked to my HR director, who knew Jamie and liked the idea. So I told Jamie I would hire her on one condition: she had to put 15 percent of her salary into a Roth IRA. She responded that she was now an adult and would make her own decisions. Good for her. Jamie joined MH Equipment and decided to put 15 percent of her salary in a Roth IRA. It is a beautiful thing when you have all the power!

Jamie did get another job outside of MH within a year and is still putting 15 percent into her Roth IRA.

Why is it difficult for people to embrace the principles we've just presented?

- Avoid accumulation of debt
- Never carry a balance on your credit card
- Live below your level of income
- Manage your debit and ATM cards
- Live on one income so you have a choice to stay at home with children if you have them
- As your salary increases, increase your rate of giving
- Set yourself up to not be a financial burden in your older age

I know sometimes there are specific circumstances outside of one's control that make it difficult to fully follow these principles, but in general I believe the answer lies with *the heart*. As Jesus said, "Where your treasure is, there will your heart be also."

But you can take austerity too far. I learned this first-hand. Let me tell you a short story about how I almost died trying to save $20.

CHAPTER 18

NEVER DIE AN IDIOT

Sometimes I think my goals in life are way too basic.

Even though MH Equipment has had a long period of success, as I've told you, my overall business goal has always simply been "Don't go bankrupt."

Similarly, one of my primary goals in all of life is this: "Don't die an idiot." Seriously, the one thing I want to avoid more than anything else is having people say after I'm gone, "Wow, what an idiot." It's like that joke about what rednecks say about themselves: "What are the last two words said before a redneck dies? Watch this!" Ha ha.

Reading about the untimely death of people has helped me to develop this goal—like the woman who was driving in bad weather. A semi was not going fast enough for her, so she sped up, passed the semi, turned around and gave the truck driver the finger. That's when she lost control of the car, spun out of control and was hit by the semi and killed. That is truly a terrible story, but I couldn't keep from thinking those four words: don't die an idiot.

Actually, the first time this concept really came home to me was when I was traveling for work. It was sometime in the early 2000s, after we had purchased the Indiana territory to represent Hyster. My standards for a hotel back then were kind of low: if it had clean sheets (actually clean was optional), cable TV to watch sports and a shower, I was good. I'll admit 1 have some false perverted pride around this, often bragging to anyone how little I spent on a hotel. (I still try to get the best deal possible.)

In Indianapolis, I chose to spend the night at a flea-ridden, run down hotel in a not so nice part of town. I believe the rate was $5 an hour or $24 for the entire night (I trust you get the drift). I could tell the environment was a little dicey: there was a lot of movement in the parking lot and people going in and out of rooms. The walls were paper thin and even though the door had a lock on it, I was pretty sure a decent kick would break it down. For the first time in my life, I was scared about the room I was staying in, so I put two chairs up against the door and moved the desk in front of the door.

All night long I was thinking, "I could get killed here
—*tonight*." Then I started thinking about how it would be
reported in the newspaper. Something like this:

*"John Wieland, CEO and Owner of MH Equipment, reasonably
wealthy individual, was murdered at a run down, flea-ridden,
drug-infested hotel all in the attempt to save $20. WHAT AN
IDIOT!"*

That's the night I really committed to trying to avoid
dying like an idiot.

While I haven't gone straight from the Dollar Inn to the
Ritz Carlton, the advent of websites that get you a better
hotel for a cheaper rate has helped me to save money
while also staying safe.

Areas where I feel I could die an idiot besides the hotels I've already mentioned:

- Excessive speeding in bad weather
- Texting while driving
- Being someplace where I shouldn't
- My last words being "Watch this"
- Taking a selfie by a cliff

I guess you could say that my secret may be to keep your overarching goals in both business and life low. And why not? You can only exceed your expectations.

CHAPTER 19

YOU CAN ONLY GIVE WHAT YOU GOT

To many people, "Take care of yourself" sounds like a very selfish statement. They believe we should be serving others, caring for others and giving to others. While that is all true, here is another truth: you can only give to people what you possess.

I've written a lot about culture and values from a business perspective. Culture is what naturally flows out of an organization, not what words on the wall say about it. A business can fake a culture, especially when circumstances are good. But when it gets more challenging, whatever is inside the organization is going to come out.

The same is true about every person that ever lived. Each of us have a personal culture; it is what naturally flows out of us.

"Naturally" is the key word here. When things are going well for me, I, like most people, can be patient and kind, gracious and funny. But shake me up and see what I do. It's what I do then that's "natural"—it's what is in me.

Let's say I have a bottle. On the outside I can put a label on it that says anything I want. But when the bottle is shaken, whatever is inside will come out, and the name on the outside won't matter. If the bottle says "water" on the outside but there is soda on the inside, we know what is going to come out of the bottle.

I am definitely more consistent and stable than I have been in the past, but when my life is shaken up, it is clear I have some ways to go. A few years ago, I went to Chicago to meet with someone to discuss my speaking at the Governor's Prayer Breakfast in Springfield. We planned to meet at the Cracker Barrel at 5 pm, and I was pretty excited about the opportunity.

My biggest pet peeve is being late for an appointment, leaving someone sitting there waiting for me. (I think this is related to my pride.) So I gave myself a half-hour cushion, leaving from Indianapolis and taking highway I65 to I80. Big mistake! The traffic was nonexistent because no one was moving. As I was getting more and more worked up, I took an exit and tried a different route. No help! I took another exit, also no help. Anyone who saw me driving would have thought I was singing or shouting to heavy metal music, but the radio was not on. Let's just say that it was not very impressive behavior.

When I arrived a half hour late and apologized profusely, the guy said, "No big deal. I was just reading a book until you got here." He didn't seem to mind the wait.

On my way home, I thanked God for the experience because it showed me what was still in me. I haven't arrived as a laidback cool guy and am instead a guy who can still go off if things don't go my way. Not going off all the time has become more of a habit, but on those occasions when I get shaken up, I thank God for giving me a glimpse of progress (or lack thereof) of "what naturally flows out of me."

Another time I was driving with my son Josiah to Taylor University to pick up his belongings. I had decided to drive a van 500 miles (the amount of money I spent on gas was worth more than the "stuff" we brought home). While Josiah was sleeping, I decided to go through Bible verses I had memorized. I was quoting 2 Corinthians 5:14, which starts out, "For the love of Christ controls us…" No sooner did I say those words than a car shifted to my lane, causing me to tap my brakes. My immediate thought was, "What an idiot." There you have it. I didn't know that if you were controlled by the love of Christ, you would quickly call strangers idiots because they slightly inconvenienced you. I continue to work at moving my head knowledge to heart knowledge. I thanked God for once again showing me my heart. I also had a pretty big smile on my face thinking about the timing of this incident.

So you need to have what you need in order to give to someone else. Think about it. If you ask me for $10 and I have $20 in my pocket, I could give you $10. If you ask me for $10 and I am dead broke, I may want to give you $10, but I can't because I don't have it to give. (Our government should listen to that!)

If I have a glass of water and someone asks me for some water, I could say yes. If I'm sitting there with an empty glass and someone asks me for some water, I do not have the ability to give them water.

Every day two things always happen: deposits and withdrawals. We are depositing physical, mental, emotional, spiritual and relational resources into our being. The key is whether they are positive or negative deposits. The best way to make sure that you are making good deposits is to have good habits in all areas of your life.

Secondly, we are also making withdrawals from the physical, mental, emotional, spiritual and relational resources from our being every day. Some of the resources are freely given while other times they come out because life gets shaken.

Going with this premise, what goes in must come out. It is critical that we are strategic and proactive in making these deposits because at the end of the day you can only give what you got.

How are you filling your barrel in the following five areas?

- Physical. Being physically healthy provides you with more productive hours in your business. If you do not control your body, your body is going to control you. If something tastes good, your body will want to experience that taste again and again, regardless of the amount you have already consumed. In general, if someone is not fit, the world makes an immediate judgment about whether or not that person has self-discipline. The way you manage your physical being will go a long way in determining your health and ability to enjoy the rest of your life.

- Mental. Being mentally sharp is important in life and business and understanding the latest trends in particular industries is key to that. Once I graduated from college, I decided that I was officially done reading, with the exception of the Bible. I figured I'd had to read a lot in college, so I didn't need to read anymore. This lasted for about five years—until a friend said to me, "John, if you are not reading, you are getting dumber by the day!" I thought, "I need new friends." Then he explained that we lose hundreds of thousands of our brain cells a day. So the math is simple: if you are not putting new thoughts and knowledge in your brain, it will slowly drain your base of knowledge. I understood the math and started to read. It doesn't matter what your continuing education looks like; the critical point is to have it.

- Emotional. In business, your EQ (Emotional Quotient, or the ability to use your emotions in a positive way) may be even more important than your IQ (Intelligence Quotient). If you're not emotionally stable, it can create incredible stress in terms of your well-being. And emotional competence is becoming an increasing concern for the current generation that's growing up with electronics. Being able to simply sit and talk is now a strength, and the ability to do so is the beginning of EQ. I ask customers for their stories because I enjoy learning from them but I also love that hearing them increases our intimacy. When someone shares their story, it takes a relationship to a different level. There is a caveat though: if the someone doesn't authentically want to hear someone's story, the relationship will not go to a different level. It would, in fact, be *no* relationship.

- Spiritual. We are spiritual beings, and what we believe about our spirit forms our worldview and influences how we respond to things. Even with my faults and failures, my spiritual guide (Christianity) has influenced me more than any other area of my physical, mental, emotional and relational life. I read my Bible probably 364 out of 365 days a year. Why the commitment? There was a time in my life that I didn't read the Bible for a few days. It turned into a few weeks, then a few months, then five years. When I got away from being nourished by my spiritual food, my outlook and behavior hit the lowest levels of my life.

- Relational. Do you steal time from your family for work? Do you steal time from your family for hobbies? Not many of us time from our

hobbies or work for our family. At MH, we let all
employees know that we have our job to support
our family, not vice versa. Employees are
pleasantly surprised to discover that we are
usually very accommodating with family issues.
If I had a family issue, I don't think I would let
work stand in the way of me addressing it. And
if it is important for me to be able to address
family issues, shoudn't all employees be able to
do the same? This is another reason why we give
our employees the opportunity to attend the
Family Life Marriage Conferences. If you are in
the midst of disaster at home, it can have a
tremendous impact on the rest of your life.

There's some truth to the adage that "a company is
only as strong as its weakest link." There is also some truth
if that adage is applied to a person, which is to say that a
person is only as strong as their weakest link—whether
that's physical, mental, emotional, spiritual or relational.
Of course, this isn't always an absolute truth. If you have a
great mind but are a train wreck emotionally, it doesn't
mean you can't do great things. But it does mean that the
weaker part of your person will diminish the strength to
some degree.

Remember what goes in will ultimately come out, and
that will also be called your legacy.

It's natural for people to want to be remembered after
they're gone; some have even done terrible things for that
reason. We are on this earth for a period of time and most

of us would like to feel we made the world a better place. I'm no different; I would love to be remembered for any accomplishments MH Equipment has had, or for some nice things Julie and I have done. We would like to leave a legacy.

But there's a difference between legacy and fame. If someone is famous, people may say they left a legacy, but that isn't necessarily true.

Fame is how long and how widespread you are known or remembered.

There are a few challenges with fame. First of all, it is tough to be remembered, period.

For example:

Can you name a person from the eighth century?

Or the 13th century?

Or who won the Super Bowl three years ago?

Or who won the MVP in baseball last year?

Or who was Hillary Clinton's running mate?

The second challenge with fame is that not everyone can be famous; if everyone is famous, of course, no one is famous. It is for the select few, so most of us don't have a shot.

By contrast, *legacy is how much your life influences your current and succeeding generations.* And the thing about legacy is that everyone has one—either good or bad.

Bill Gates is famous, but his legacy will far outlive his fame. He's been instrumental in changing how we do life in business and at home. In the year 2121, most people will not remember the name Bill Gates, but their life will still be influenced by him. Thomas Edison, Benjamin Franklin, Alexander Graham Bell, the Wright Brothers, Henry Ford, Johannes Gutenberg, Steve Jobs, Galileo and the list goes on of inventors and pioneers whose legacy endures. But as the years go by, these names will be less known.

As I think about my legacy, I've concluded that in 200 years, MH Equipment will not exist. Therefore, even though MH Equipment has provided decent employment for thousands of families over the years, I hope my legacy will be more personal.

When Mother Teresa ministered to those dying of AIDS in Calcutta, India, she challenged the world to be a little nicer, a littler warmer. People throughout the world have pursued a life of service because of her example.

A lesser-known person, Jim Elliot, had a vision to share the Love and Teachings of Christ with the Auca Indians in Ecuador. On the fateful day of January 8, 1956, they landed at the village, expecting the sort of positive greeting that they had worked to create previously. Instead of the friendly greeting, 10 warriors killed Jim and four other missionaries. The story rocked the world. A 29-year-old man and four others' lives were wasted.

But something significant happened. The death of Jim and the others caused the missionary movement in the late 1950s to explode in a way that is still being felt. In fact, Jim's widow, Elizabeth, returned to the village that killed her husband for years of fruitful ministry.

These are the stories on which legacies are made. But there is a catch.

Many of us want to do great things for God like Jim Elliot or Mother Teresa, but it's crucial to be careful of our motivation. My prayer at one time was, "Lord, I want to do great things for Your kingdom. God, if you want me to speak to crowds of hundreds and thousands, I will. And if some people come up to me and say I inspired them, I will humbly try to deflect the compliments to You. That is just part of the territory when you do Great things for God." Maybe that prayer reveals more about my desire to be famous than about expanding the Glory of God.

This is what I want my prayer to be today: "God, use me any way you want that will bring You glory, even if it is cleaning the wounds of dying AIDS patients in Calcutta and no one knows I even exist." Yes, Mother Teresa became famous, but there are many others the world never knew who did the exact same thing. Do you think God gives more credit to Mother Teresa than those the world knows nothing about? God is not very interested in our personal fame!

Consider this relevant fact: the 12 disciples who began Christianity are 12 really important people, but three of these disciples are only mentioned in the Bible when the 12 are mentioned as a group and nowhere else. As Jesus's fame grew, those three disciples became a footnote. Do you think they were the losers of the group? It is fame that has to do with being remembered, not legacy. Church history says those three were martyred in expanding the Gospel just like most of the others.

In actuality, it isn't the great things but the small things that produce a legacy.

Many of those who follow Christ are used by Him without much fanfare, but they definitely are creating a legacy.

My mom is a great example of someone who lived under the radar but still created a legacy—a legacy of "grace and mercy." Her children, grandchildren and great-grandchildren have been influenced not just by her words but by her daily touches that reflected grace and mercy into our lives. The little conversations, the needed encouragements, the timely hugs and prayers. The amazing thing about legacy is that it is not just a gift you leave for your loved ones when you die; they are already benefiting from it while you are living.

High-profile people can leave legacies and Average Joe's can leave a legacy, but there is another group. Hebrews 11 gives a list of people that God pats on the back for being faithful. It's a fascinating list of people.

For example, a prostitute is on the list: Rahab. The only thing she did was fear the God of Israel and hide the spies when they came to Jericho; plus, she lied about it. Yet, she is on the list. What does that tell you? That God can use any one of us when we act on our faith—even someone like Rahab, an embarrassment to the family. Rahab didn't have much in her life but because of what she did with it, God honored her.

We all want to have respectable names in our community. But in truth, it is a house of cards. Most families will have multiple divorces, members in rehab or prison or who just don't amount to much. But this is the beauty of God; the one we may be a little disappointed by could be the one God uses to expand His Kingdom in a miraculous way that gives the family name the highest honor, just like Rahab.

This is one of the reasons I love God. Even though the world may give up on you, God never does. He created you for a reason.

God gives talents to everyone—some a lot, some a little. And His pleasure is not based on the absolute number of talents, but what we actually did with the few talents He gave us. We have a High Priest that is able to sympathize with our weaknesses. He understands, He forgives, He restores, He redeems—even the least of us, if we only reach out to Him.

I am pretty sure what is true about me is true about you. Whatever legacy we may have will be things we did or said that we don't even remember doing. They are the little touches, the consistency of behavior, the times spent on our knees. Contribute to humanity and rest assured you will leave a legacy.

PART III

FAITH

I left this section for last for one simple reason: its influence is massive. Whatever faith you have, it is the foundation of your worldview; faith guides us in our understanding of how the world ought to be. Atheists have a worldview that drives their behavior just as much as all religious people of the world. If someone's worldview is that everything is fair game and how you get it doesn't really matter, it has a tremendous impact on how their family and business play out.

In this last section, I share my faith journey. I have had good moments when I love and serve Him well. And I have moments I reflect anything but the Spirit of God. Whether in success or failure, faith lessons help me grow. Faith has taught me to stay on level ground. Faith has taught me that I don't have to have every single thing figured out before I go for something. Faith provides me with a level of contentment and peace even when things are in chaos. Think about a leader that you would be willing to follow. A leader that doesn't think too highly of themself? A leader that doesn't need all the answers to go forward? A leader that is at peace with his God and the world? I can't think of a better leader.

Faith is the final piece of the triangle.

CHAPTER 20

A MATURE CHRISTIAN VERSUS A DRUNK TEENAGER

As I've said, I became a follower of Jesus my second year of college and married Julie four years later. I wish I could tell you the story of how I bowed the knee so many years ago and have lived a righteous life ever since, how I have honored Julie all the years of our marriage and how I have kept myself unstained from this world. But I can't.

I had an experience that really brought to light how I was losing my way. Back in the day, I went to my high school 20th class reunion. In high school, I wasn't a follower of Jesus Christ. In fact, high school life was about pushing the limits in everything. Living across the street from the school and having a pool in the back yard meant that big parties were common. I drank a lot, partied a lot and was completely immoral when it came to the opposite sex. It was when I came to faith in college that I started to get my life headed in a different direction.

When I went to my 20th high school reunion, I knew I was blessed. I had a wife who loved me, three children at the time and I owned a little company. I was a different person than I was in high school, and I wanted my classmates at this 20th reunion to know I had changed for the better. I was a Christian.

As I walked around, a couple of classmates came up and told me that one of our former classmates, Debbie, was looking for me and, by the way, she was wearing a black leather miniskirt and nothing but a bikini top for the rest of her clothing. We joked that I needed to avoid her. Julie was with me, and she had already heard enough incriminating stories about my past. I really didn't want to relive another one.

Two more times people came up to me, saying, "Have you seen the way Debbie is dressed? And by the way she is asking for you!" Each time, we joked about how I needed to avoid that conversation. You see, Debbie lived on the fringe. She hung around the down-and-outers, didn't get good grades and made bad choices. Most of us were surprised she would show up at a class reunion.

Debbie finally found me and yes, she was dressed as advertised.

"Hi Debbie," I said.

"Hi John," she replied. "I have wanted to tell you something for 20 years."

I had no idea what this was about or what she was going to say. What would someone hold on to for 20 years just to tell someone they saw at a reunion? Rifling through my memory, I couldn't recall doing something so bad that she would hang on to it for 20 years. So I asked, "What's that, Debbie?"

Debbie went on to drop this bombshell: "John, what I've waited 20 years to simply say to you is…thank you! You were the only popular guy in school that treated me like a real person."

All I could say was "Thanks, Debbie," and then I walked away. I was devastated. I basically trashed her three times that night when all she wanted to do was say, "Thanks for being nice."

I don't ever remember spending time with Debbie, but evidently she felt welcomed at my stupid parties and if she said hi to me when I was with my buddies, I wouldn't embarrass her. Somehow, she felt I included her.

Yes, I had changed, and I told a whole lot of people I was a follower of Jesus Christ. And it was at that point I realized that I'd demonstrated the genuine heart of Jesus to the least and the lost more authentically 20 years earlier as a drunk, amoral teenager than I did that night.

So what went wrong? There was no question I bowed the knee when I was at college. I knew the foot of the Cross was not only the place I found salvation, but it was also the place to live in peace. But slowly, this process occurred.

God gave me Julie. Thank You, Jesus. I'm married. I took a step on the ladder of success.

God gave me children. Thank You, Jesus. I'm a father. I took another step on the ladder of success.

God gave me a company. Thank You, Jesus. I own a business. I took another step on the ladder of success.

God blessed me. Thank You, Jesus. I am Somebody.

I had taken all of Jesus's Blessings and started to process them as though I was the center of the universe. I even said, "Thank You, Jesus," but quickly returned to centering my attention on me.

And now it is pretty hard to kneel at the Cross when you are halfway up a ladder.

What I should have said is this:

You gave me Julie. Thank You, Jesus. I commit her to you.

You gave me children. Thank You, Jesus. I commit them to you.

You gave me a little business. Thank You, Jesus. I commit it to you.

You have blessed me. Thank You, Jesus. I commit *all* to You.

But like I said, that is not my story. I have been up and down that ladder too many times to count. I've been up those rungs because of sin and also by taking the good things of God and making them about myself. The old hymn is so right; we are "prone to wander." With each additional step, it gets easier to walk away from the Cross. And it is on this ladder that my life blows up and I come crashing down, back to the Cross, crying like a baby, only to take another step later.

From a business perspective, it is much easier when you live at the Cross.

I keep learning—stay close to the Cross!

CHAPTER 21

IN THE HANDS OF THE MIRACLE MAN

If I had to wait until I was sure that everything was in perfect order and I had everything I needed for success, this book would simply not exist. I didn't have enough skills or experience or even money. I needed some help.

In the Gospel of John, there is a powerful story about doing much with very little.

Philip was one of the Apostles and he was excited about finding the Messiah. He was so excited he told another future Apostle Nathaneal, "Come, look, we have found the Messiah!" He had so much faith that he left his business to follow Him.

But in John 6, when Jesus fed the 5,000, Jesus—already knowing what He was going to do—tested Philip and asked him what they should do. Philip looked at the current resources and said, "We can't feed these people, so let's send them home." Philip had become a professing Christian but a practicing atheist, and his response was no different than an unbeliever's. Philip made decisions based on what Philip could do with the resources in his hand, not with what Jesus could do.

Andrew, on the other hand, found a young child with two small fish and five loaves of bread and brought them to Jesus. He knew in his hand it was nothing, but in the hand of the Miracle Man, who knows? Philip saw the miracle but missed out on exercising his faith. He was on the sidelines that day, and his faith struggled until the resurrection.

It has been said that a lot of people who go to church live like they're professing Christians and practicing atheists. What does living by faith look like? Faith is simply the gap between what you have and what it takes to succeed.

Here are a few examples of how people don't have everything they need to succeed but took that step of faith.

When our kids were growing up, I would often take them to and from school. On the way, I would ask one of them to pray. One time I picked Jamie to pray, but she didn't want to. I told her I didn't care and to start praying. She began to pray, "mumble mumble mumble." In my righteous anger I yelled, "Jamie, how do you think God feels when I ask you to pray and He can't even hear you?" Incredible display of parenting.

We sat there in dead silence as I basked in the glory of my self-righteousness. That was until my troublemaking daughter Jennifer spoke up.

"Dad, I don't mean to be sassy, but how do you think God feels when you yell at your daughter about not praying loud enough for Him to hear?"

The only thing I could say was "You may have a point

there." There was no more noise to be heard on the way to school except the sounds of Jessica and Josiah giving Jennifer high fives in the back seat.

Jesus is real to Jennifer. She was in fifth grade the day I yelled at Jamie for not praying loud enough, and even though Jennifer didn't have much strength on her side, she gave her fish and loaves to God, spoke truth and in the meantime gave her father a good old fashioned "throw down." Her faith grew because she was a practicing Christian.

I had to take a step of faith when it came to speaking, let alone public speaking. The odds of me ever speaking to an audience weren't very good. When I was in elementary school my parents took me to a speech pathologist because I had difficulty sounding out words. English didn't get any easier for me in high school. When I took my ACT test in high school, I scored an impressive 9 on my English exam. I still butcher the English language, my grammar is painful to listen to and my voice is not the deep majestic one people like to hear. Keep this to yourselves, but on multiple occasions when I've stayed at hotels, I've called the front desk and asked some snot-nosed kid to give me a wakeup call. And in a matter of seconds this attendant completely emasculates me. This is how it goes: "Can I have a wakeup call for 6 am?" He responds, "Yes ma'am, is there anything else?" What do I do? I can't argue with the person. So I do what any other self-respecting man would do. I raise my voice slightly and say, "Thank you." I then watch Ultimate Fighting for a half hour in order to reassure myself of my manhood.

The point is even with defective fish and loaves, God can give Grace.

There was this guy who worked at the gas station across the street from our church. He looked like he was from the Middle East and he didn't smile. He had big bushy eyebrows and actually looked kind of mean. When he looked at you, he kind of bent his head down. This was shortly after 9/11, and I didn't have a desire to get to know him. I had biases!

My wife, on the other hand, had started talking to him when she went in for gas and found out his name was Persima and that she shared her love for Jesus. She ended up giving him several booklets to read. She is always doing things like that. If you're a plumber, electrician, carpenter, painter or someone doing yard work who comes to our house, Julie will share the Gospel with you. I know some of you guys may be thinking at this moment, boy, it appears John is completely worthless around the house, but that is not my point! Julie gave her fish and loaves to God and trusted God would do something. and a couple of months later, Julie told me Persima accepted Jesus as his Savior. Julie's faith grew because she was a practicing Christian. I was left holding on to empty biases.

There were major gaps for me when I took on a virtually bankrupt company at the age of 35 with little net worth, no mechanical skills in the company's industry and no real leadership experience. I worked hard to close the gap but still I had to take a step of faith.

Just like the story of the two fish and the five loaves, when we place our talents (however few) into His Hands, amazing things can happen.

CHAPTER 22

LASTING CONTENTMENT

Most of us can agree on the fact that we would like contentment. But contentment doesn't mean you become lazy or have no ambition or you don't want to improve things; it means that when you put your head on your pillow and close your eyes, you have peace.

When Josiah was about five years old, we liked wrestling each other. At that time, I would flip him on top of me, ask him who was winning and he would say, "Josiah!" Then I would flip so I was on top of him, ask him who was winning and he would say "Dad!" Then I would move us where we were side by side and ask him who was winning and he would say "TIE!" Josiah would run upstairs and then come back downstairs for another round. I never knew why he did that until I followed him. He actually had a score card and would mark when he won or lost. One time while we were playing, Josiah looked up and said through his laughter, "Daddy's boy."

I realized at that moment, Josiah was completely content simply being my son. *Who* he was was defined by *whose* he was. That was one great day for me. As a father I knew I couldn't keep that stature in the eyes of my son forever. Actually, it ended the next day when Josiah told me I disgusted him!

But that blessed day with Josiah reminded me of something else. Did you know that three times in the New Testament the term *Abba Father* is used, which in our language means "Daddy"? Romans 8:15 says: *"But you have received adoption as sons by which we cry out, 'Abba Father.'"* [1] When was the last time I was with my Heavenly Father and had such intimacy that I cried out "Daddy's Boy"? I needed to look into that.

Jesus had some special things to say about children:

People were bringing little children to Jesus to have Him touch them, but the disciples rebuked them. When Jesus saw this, He was indignant. He said to them, "Let the little children come to me, and do not hinder them, for the kingdom of God belongs to such as these. I tell you the truth, anyone who will not receive the kingdom of God like a little child will never enter it."[2]

It doesn't say "Consider coming like a child" or "When you are a child." Nope. It says "Come as a child." He is speaking to a group of all ages, even the elderly. As I think about this verse and the story of Josiah, I believe there is a connection.

So often as we get older and know more of the Bible, we think the relationship with our Father in Heaven becomes more peer-like in nature. That may be true with our earthly father but not our Heavenly Father. Even though we were created in the image of God, the fact is we are still the created just like all other creation, and we need to come to the realization that we have a closer peer relationship with a maggot than with the God and Creator of the universe.

The more I study the Bible, the more I see that there is one person who seemed to have a great intimacy and childlike love for his Father in Heaven: King David.

In the book of Acts it says of David; *"God testified concerning him: 'I have found David, son of Jesse, a man after my own heart; he will do everything I want him to do.'"*[3]

As David grew in power, his relationship with God never turned into a peer relationship. David knew who he was and knew who God was. He wasn't the holiest, smartest, strongest or bravest. But there was no question he had a passionate love for His Father in Heaven. His understanding that he was his "Father's son" was always at the forefront of who he was. His identity was never in *who* he was but *whose* he was.

In the book of Psalms, we see David praying to his Father:

"Keep me as the apple of your eye; hide me in the shadow of your wings."[4]

Any parent knows exactly what it means for a child to be the "apple of your eye." That was David's heart's desire. Also, David wanted to be "hid in the shadow of God"—he wanted the shadow of God to swallow him up so that people would see his Heavenly Father and not him. Just think about that for a moment. Here was David—the most powerful person in the entire world—and he wanted to be hidden in the shadow of God so people would just see his Dad. In sad contrast, I, on the other hand—like others—really do want to be known and seen. In fact, my wife says I have a serious case of ADD: if people don't show me enough attention, I create disorder.

But not David. This is why David was highly esteemed by God. If you had asked David at the height of his power who he was, he would have said, "I am a son of the One True God," long before saying he was king. That was his primary identity. That was his purpose. To *be* a son of The Father.

King David struggled in life as much as anyone. He committed adultery, tried to do the cover-up thing, killed the husband, took a census of the Israelites, which was forbidden, and so on. But throughout David's life, when he sinned, instead of hiding from God, he came running to his Dad and poured his heart out. Some may be thinking that this is a little soft theologically, but I want to be very clear on this: for a believer, the depth of repentance is directly related to the depth of love you have for the one you have offended. You love God a little, you repent a little. You love God a lot, you repent a lot. When David committed adultery and his sin was put before him, it was out of his love for his Father that he penned the very famous Psalm 51:

> *Wash away all my iniquity and cleanse me from my sin. For I know my transgressions, and my sin is always before me. Against you, you only, have I sinned and done what is evil in your sight . . . Create in me a clean heart, O God, and renew a right spirit within me. Cast me not away from your presence O Lord, and take not Holy Spirit from me. Restore unto me the joy of thy salvation and renew a right spirit within me.* [5]

Are there consequences for sin? Absolutely! There are natural, physical, relational, emotional and spiritual consequences, and they can be painful (I have had my share). But the Bible says God disciplines those He loves, and He disciplines for our growth and benefit, not because He has had enough of us. Our sin and God's love are not connected. The passion of His love for His children does not rise and fall based on our behavior. Every other relationship we have has some performance requirement, but not with our Father in Heaven. We have fellowship with the Father through the

Cross of Christ. But when we sin, what do we so often do? We want to get away from the Cross to try to clean things up on our own and then come back. How dysfunctional is that? The One Power given to us to overcome the corruption of this world is the very power we run away from when we most need it. So when we stumble and fall, we need to run to the Father who loves us unconditionally. I know that the more I think about being His son, the less attractive the sin of this world is.

Lasting contentment comes from knowing and embracing your life purpose. I believe for each of us, young or old, it is first and foremost simply being "Daddy's Boy" or "Daddy's Girl."

I'm one of the lucky ones. I had a father on earth I knew loved me and accepted me even at my lowest points in life. The idea of a loving Father was not a long road for me. But some people may be saying something like, "John, you don't understand. I hate my father, nothing I ever did was good enough for that man. Nothing. I got a B, it should have been an A. I scored 8 points in a game and he said it should have been 12. Nothing was ever good enough. I have no interest in being Daddy's Boy or Daddy's Girl."

Or: "John, my dad was a stinking drunk. He embarrassed me and my family all the time. He left me and my mom—alone, helpless, hopeless—for another woman. He was gone when I most needed him. A Father? NO THANK YOU!"

Or: "My dad 'died on me' and I carry that sorrow every

day and I never want sorrow like that again. We are fine without a Father."

The fact that people know what the negative attributes of a Father are confirms that people know the opposite is the Father they desire. A Father who accepts you for simply being you, a Father who won't leave you, a Father who will protect you, restore you, give you hope, a Father who will be faithful and true.

The Father in Heaven is a great and awesome Father. Throughout the Holy Scriptures we see many wonderful attributes of our Heavenly Father:

He is slow to anger, compassionate, abounding in love. He is faithful to all His promises. He will give us a Hope and a Future. He will make straight our paths. He watches over us. He is the Chief Shepherd and cares for His flock. He goes before us, He never leaves or forsakes us. He is near to us when we call, He hears our prayers. He will give us rest for our souls. He knew us before we were conceived. He knows the number of hairs on our head. We are His treasured possession.

He is Faithful and True. He is patient, gracious, merciful and kind. He is our refuge in times of trouble. He protects us from the enemy. He encourages the downcast. He holds up the afflicted. He redeems us from our sin.

He is the Father to the fatherless, the Defender of the defenseless, the Hope to the hopeless, the Mender of a broken heart.

He knows everything about us, and still He loves us. Neither death nor life, neither angels nor demons, neither the present nor the future nor any powers, neither height nor depth nor anything else in all creation will be able to separate us from the Love of this Father!

There is one more thing this Father has done. When man rebelled against him, was His enemy and had nothing to offer, this Father sent His Son to the Cross for you and me so we could have this relationship. The day I bowed at this Cross, the Father nailed my sin, my pride, my shame to this Cross. And I am His forevermore.

It is this God, this Father, this Daddy whose boy I desperately want to be!

When people ask you to tell them about yourself, how long will it take for you to say "I'm Daddy's boy, or Daddy's girl"? It took two seconds for a five-year-old boy named Josiah to teach me that lesson for a lifetime. Lasting contentment does not happen by doing, it happens by being—by resting in that Love relationship with your Creator and Father!

CHAPTER 23

SO YOU WANT TO TAKE JESUS TO THE OFFICE

Many people like to take their faith and give it to the world, regardless of what that faith is. It is called proselytizing. In many corners of the world, the idea of sharing your beliefs can be out and out offensive. But if you think it through, proselytizing is very logical.

Atheist Penn Jillette, of the magician duo Penn & Teller, actually explains why it is so logical. "I've always said that I don't respect people who don't share their beliefs," he said. "I don't respect that at all. If you believe that there's a heaven and a hell, and people could be going to hell or not getting eternal life, and you think that it's not really worth telling them this because it would make it socially awkward—and atheists who think people shouldn't share their beliefs and who say just leave me alone and keep your religion to yourself—how much do you have to hate somebody to *not* share your beliefs? How much do you have to hate somebody to believe everlasting life is possible and not tell them that? I mean, if I believed, beyond the shadow of a doubt, that a truck was coming at you, and you didn't believe that truck was bearing down on you, there is a certain point where I tackle you. And this is *more* important than that."

I agree with much of what Penn said. When, as a college sophomore, I became a follower of Jesus, I became pretty zealous for the Kingdom. I grew up going to church, but it was more of a custom than something personal. But in college, I ran multiple Bible studies, participated in Athletes in Action with karate demonstrations and, as a resident assistant, worked to create an environment where it was easy to have spiritual conversations.

Through my work life, I have had various experiences when it's come to sharing my faith. I have seen fruit and I have had many failures. I've come up with a few things that are really important to do, if you want to be effective in sharing your faith. I've discovered more than a few things not to do if you want to bear fruit.

Don't Suck at Your Job

I mean it. Don't suck at your job. If you are a lousy employee, your credibility is significantly damaged. When a company employs you, it is a contract. They will pay you money, and in turn you will perform duties assigned. Perform these duties with excellence. It drives me up a wall when I see a Christian slack at the office or in their job. Christians are told they do not work for man but for the King of Kings. Understanding who you ultimately work for should be plenty of motivation to serve well even if your earthly boss is not a good boss at all. I believe that Christians should be the most reliable and trustworthy employees in a company. Sadly, much of the time, they are not.

Employers love great employees. Not only do they love them but they will also accommodate or tolerate behavior they may not embrace. At KPMG, I know for a fact I wasn't the fan favorite of all the bosses. When they wanted 100 percent participation for the United Way Campaign, I declined because of their support of Planned Parenthood (United Way is a fine organization, and I don't think there is a right or wrong answer on supporting them; it comes down to the individual). The bosses were frustrated, but if they had a job and I was available, they quickly picked me. I typically got the job done under budget with sufficient quality, and the bosses made more money.

There was a time I was having a Bible study before work in the conference room. The big boss at the time called me in the office and questioned the fact that I was hosting the study on work premises. In a polite way, I asked if there would be a problem if a book club was using the conference room before work. To his credit, he thought about that and decided the studies were okay. Still, the reason he was open to my suggestion was surely related to the fact that he liked to have me on his jobs. (This boss also agreed to be on my board when I bought MH years later!)

Don't Steal From the Company

An employee can steal time or money.

As a missionary, it's crucial not to steal time from your employer. You know how much the culture of your company allows for general conversation during the day, so don't exceed it.

If I put a pen in my pocket from work and then forget about it, and it ends up at my house, I don't think that is stealing. If you take a box of pens, paper and toilet paper home with you, that is a different story. But how you handle commerce has a great impact on how people perceive you.

Back at KPMG, we had a job out of town where we had to spend the night in a hotel. When employees spent the night out of town, they would get a per diem of $25 a day, broken down for breakfast, lunch and dinner. The dinner portion was $12. One night the owners of the company we were auditing asked us to their house for a big chicken dinner. It was a great dinner, and we were stuffed. When it came down to filling out my expense report, I questioned whether I should include the $12 for the dinner. I mean, it wasn't clear, but in my gut, I felt I shouldn't. Well, I included it and requested the full $25. The guy who was in charge of the job and who was at the dinner confronted me.

"John, why did you ask for the $12 for dinner?" he asked. "It was provided to you for free. I thought you were a Christian."

For a grand total of $12, I harmed my ability to share what it means to be Christian to my boss.

Be Kind and Respectful, Not Warm and Cozy

Being warm and cozy to the opposite sex is a dangerous road, and it is especially dangerous for extroverts like me. The distance between being warm and cozy and flirting is very short and most of the time, it does cross over to flirting. Flirting has a whole other set of problems. When you're married or the person that you're flirting with is married, your coworkers will surely consider you a hypocrite. When you go to one cubicle and talk about Jesus, and then you go to the next cubicle and flirt, your credibility to share your faith evaporates.

Kind and respectful is the sure road and leads to consistency between your walk and talk. As part of the male species, I do much better when the opposite sex treats me with kindness and respect. Lines do not get blurred.

I am sure there are people that are warm and cozy and have a pure heart; I don't. And people that follow the guidelines can be full of bad things, just like the Pharisees in Jesus's day.

Be Honest About Your Brokenness

When I first entered the business world, I tried to hide my own brokenness. I denied that I had any issues with pride, lust, envy or pornography. I believed that coworkers care very little about what you profess until they see a walk that is consistent with what you say. I took that to mean I needed to be perfect. But while people should see something attractive in our lifestyle if we are indwelled with the Holy Spirit, that is a far cry from being perfect.

If you try to appear perfect, you are actually misrepresenting the Gospel. The Gospel is for one people group and one people group only: "broken people." When Christians act like they are no longer broken, people see through it. The Fruit of the Spirit is love, joy, peace, patience, kindness, goodness, faithfulness, gentleness and self-control. When you embrace this Fruit, you will be more consistent, but the Fruit does not include sinlessness. When I became more authentic about my own challenges in life, something clicked with those around me. People started coming to me with their own challenges—not because I have the answer or have everything together, but because I no longer judged other people's struggles, and they knew I would honestly listen to them and invest in their lives. It is through this journey that both of us can grow.

Do Not Be a One Trick Pony

If a coworker asks you what time it is, don't use that opportunity to go into a mini sermon about how God tells us to number our days! Tell the dude, "It's 4:30." You don't want to have a reputation for being the person that turns the conversation around to the spiritual every time someone talks to you. Be able to talk about a wide variety of subjects. I read books on faith, leadership, history, biographies and human behavior, among other topics. I pay attention to sports. Being well-rounded gives me the opportunity to connect with most anyone at some level.

Saying "I Don't Know" Is a Good Thing

When I first entered the business world, I was the Bible Answer Man. I had an answer for everything, even if I didn't have an answer. I was a real pain in the butt! People see right through the phoniness. And it goes a long way when someone asks you a spiritual question and your response is, "That is a good question. I don't know the answer to that!" God is Omniscient (all knowing), not you, so don't act like it. As I matured in my faith, I learned there are mysteries in all of life, especially when it comes to faith. When I quit acting like the Bible Answer Man, I began to get more questions from people and have more honest conversations. There are things that are meant to be a mystery in faith. Embrace the beauty of mystery.

Respect People's Boundaries

If you begin to proselytize in various forms to someone and they say they don't want to talk about things like that, respect the boundary. Instead of talking to them, pray for them. It is not against the law to share your faith, but in business, if someone has said "I don't want to talk about faith" and you continue to push the conversation, it turns into harassment that the person may consider to be a part of a hostile work environment.

The Ground at the Cross Is Level

One day, when I was working at KPMG at the lowest level, I went by the office of the person who was in charge of the operations and asked him how he was doing.

"Things are okay," he said. His response was not convincing.

"It doesn't seem like everything is okay," I said.

He confessed that his home life was a struggle, so I asked him if I could pray for him. He was a little taken aback but said yes. I closed his door, knelt by his desk and prayed for him and his family. Our relationship was never the same. There was a genuine bond established as we both humbled ourselves at the Cross.

Years later, when I was already the CEO of MH Equipment, a part time older employee came into my office. I welcomed her and asked what she needed. She told me that her 40-something son had cancer. She was scared and asked if we could pray for him. I stood up, went over to her, put my hand on her shoulder, and together we prayed for her son. It was meaningful for both of us. This is the essence of humanity.

Whether you are the president of the United States or a person dying of AIDS in Calcutta, the Cross of Christ is on level ground.

Get to Know Their Story

Everyone has a story, and most people tend to not mind sharing theirs. When people know you have invested in them because you want to get to know them and their story, you can have wonderfully honest conversations. In those cases, get to know their family as well as their joys and struggles. Pray for God's Grace and Mercy upon them and their family and for the work of the Holy Spirit. Be willing to share your story, too. When you get to know each other's stories, faith will come into the conversation naturally.

I can guarantee one thing that will happen in your life if you are a Christian: you will blow it from time to time. But no one expects you to be perfect. What people are looking for in you is simple honesty and humility. So next time you blow it, apologize and ask for forgiveness. People will notice!

CHAPTER 24

LESSONS LEARNED FROM A BONE MARROW TRANSPLANT

The autumn of 2018 was pretty tough for me.

My mother was in her final days, and I was diagnosed with Myelodysplastic Syndrome. My bone marrow was not producing sufficient red blood cells, which provide oxygen to the heart.

Back in 2015, I went to my primary doctor, Randolph, to get my biannual check-up. He was concerned about my hemoglobin level, which is a measure for your red blood cells. It had been in the normal range of 13 to 15 but had dropped to the mid-10s. He sent me to a hematologist at the Illinois Cancer Center. Dr. J showed the same concern and started testing my blood regularly at first, then annually. For three years, my level stayed in the mid-10 range.

But in July of 2018, my stamina was almost nonexistent, so I went in to have my blood tested and discovered my hemoglobin was now at seven. I started to receive blood transfusions and chemo but wasn't getting any better. Ultimately, I was told my condition was not sustainable. Then another provider told me I was blood transfusion dependent. Together these comments basically meant that unless I did something, I was a dead man walking. It was my friend, Dr. Andy Chiou, who convinced me to get to Mayo and address this issue. Hindsight: Andy is a good friend!

Julie and I knew we could address this in several ways. One was to take chemo shots with the hopes of increasing the good red blood cells. The challenge with this approach was that it has a shelf life: it could work for x number of years but no one knew when it would become ineffective.

Another option was to take a much more aggressive approach and have a complete bone marrow transplant, which if successful would remove the disease. Julie and I decided to pursue this treatment. On February 6, 2019, we traveled to Rochester, Minnesota to begin a three-month journey. None of my siblings were a direct match, but I was fortunate and ended up with a direct match through the bone marrow registry.

When I gathered my family together to tell them, I said, "During this journey there will be news we like and news we don't like. Don't focus on the daily news. Focus on our fundamentals. Our fundamental belief is that God is good, regardless of what happens this side of heaven." By His Grace, we really didn't have much news we didn't like. But during the journey there were some important lessons I learned.

The first lesson is that *life is not about me*, so I need to keep my eyes on others. Singer/songwriter Keith Green wrote a song called "Make My Life a Prayer to You" and in it, he sings the words "It's so hard to see when my eyes are on me." That's a great verse and great wisdom.

Julie and I decided to not be consumed with my medical condition. We have a desire to share the love of Jesus Christ and meet the physical needs of people in His Name, and during our three months in Rochester, our desire didn't change—only the location. We spent most of our time listening to stories of nurses, providers and fellow patients. We laughed and cried with them, we bought gifts for them, we prayed with and for them and we loved them. My primary doctor was a Muslim from Syria. So I bought a book on the civil war in Syria so I could talk to him about his homeland. He thought that was cool. I told him I read the Koran and did a Sunday school series on it. He thought that was cool. I was hoping he would ask me my thoughts so I could suggest a conversation as soon as he read my book, the New Testament. Actually, those three months are cherished memories.

The second thing I learned was *I have to quit thinking too highly of myself.* Julie and I started watching *Jeopardy* every day. One day I was getting half of the answers right and started to think maybe I could be on the show. As soon as I started thinking about my brilliance the next question was from the category "What type of fuel?" The answer was "NASA'S Saturn V rocket was powered by more than 700,000 gallons of hydrogen and oxygen in this state."

I shouted, "What is Florida?"

The correct answer was "What is liquid?" I guess I had

the wrong state! Julie looked at me like, "Great response, Einstein!" If I had been on live TV, it could have been disastrous for my hometown of Peoria. When people across the nation gave a stupid answer, the response would be "I take it you're from Peoria." So all of Peoria can be thankful I will never be on *Jeopardy*.

My third lesson was in *understanding prayer* a little bit better. I've questioned how prayer works or even why we pray. My prayer life has always been weak. What point is there if it is a mystery? But we are always called to pray. Prayer does influence. James says the prayer of a righteous person has great power in its effects. I just don't know how.

Isaiah wrote, "*My thoughts are not your thoughts, neither are your ways My Ways, says the Lord. As the heavens are higher than the earth, so are My Ways higher than your ways, and My Thoughts than your thoughts.*"[1] That helps a little.

But I learned that there is always a benefit in praying. It provides increased intimacy with God and those for whom you are praying. As we pray for others, our dependence on God grows. It acknowledges the order of things. We realize He is God and we are not. It creates humility in us. But another thing I found is that it increases the intimacy between the one who is praying and the one for whom I pray. As people pray for me and I for them, there is always greater intimacy.

We had over 100 prayer requests. A family grieving over their 18-year-old daughter who was killed by a drunk driver. An 11-year-old girl hearing voices in her head to hurt herself. Failing businesses. Broken marriages and broken lives. When people are honest about their fears and struggles, deeper relationships form. When people ask me how things are going, I always say, "Considering the ordinary struggle of life, things are going okay." Amazing what type of responses I get from being a little vulnerable.

You see the deepest growth when you follow up with the people for whom you are praying. One of the guys in the group I get together with monthly asked me to pray about a family matter, and so I would pray for him and ask for updates periodically. When we got together after I was in the hospital, he told the group about the prayer request. He actually broke down crying when he told the group he got a text from me asking how things were going, considering what I was going through at the time. It touched him deeply that I would be thinking and praying for him. Don't you think our friendship is just a little bit deeper after that?

I think this is a primary reason God wants us to pray for each other: to draw our community a little closer so that we love one another a little deeper, and our world becomes a little smaller, a little warmer.

This is a guarantee for us when we authentically pray for each other. Every time!

As people of faith, we trust that through the eyes of eternity, this life is truly just a moment—whether we live for one day or 100 years.

The final lesson I learned is *I am a hypocrite*. Let me explain.

I had a bone marrow transplant. They gave me a ton of chemo to kill all my bone marrow—all of it. Then I received the bone marrow of a donor. Next, I went through engrafting. If I kept my bone marrow or even some of it, I would die from it. If my body accepted the new bone marrow completely, I would live. Complete engrafting is required. I wanted this to work for obvious reasons. There were probably thousands of people that prayed for me that my old bone marrow would completely die and the new bone marrow would take 100 percent control. I prayed. I pleaded with God, along with my family, friends and people I didn't even know to let my body reflect 100 percent of the new bone marrow and have my old bone marrow eradicated from my body forever. It was a matter of physical life and death.

As a believer in Christ, I believe we are indwelled with the Holy Spirit. The Bible says we have been grafted into the Body of Christ. The new nature is the Holy Spirit creating love, joy, peace, patience, kindness, goodness, faithfulness, gentleness, self-control; against such there is no law.

The old nature is full of self-righteousness, greed, jealousy, pride and hatred. In other words, *sin.*

How often have I prayed or pleaded with God or asked people to pray my sinful nature would be eradicated from my DNA, and the Holy Spirit would reign supreme in all things at all times? The answer is not often, and I've never asked people to pray for this specific request.

We have a physical nature and a spiritual nature. We know the physical nature will ultimately pass away, but we also know the spiritual nature is eternal. I found myself more concerned about my temporary physical life than my eternal spiritual life. I actually find myself being okay with some sin. "We are all still sinners," I would think to myself.

Paul's letter to the Galatians says, *"Walk by the Spirit and do not gratify the desires of the flesh, for the flesh is against the Spirit and the Spirit is against the flesh. These two are opposed to each other to prevent you from doing what you should."*[2]

James said, *"But each man is tempted when he is lured and enticed by his own desire and desire when conceived gives birth to sin and sin when it is full grown brings forth death!"*[3]

But we live as if we don't believe it. Yet it is the written Word of God. How many marriages end in divorce? Is that not death? And how did it start? We were enticed by our own desire.

How many people have destroyed their lives with addictions? Is that not death? And how did it start? We were enticed by our own desire.

How many of us don't care for our body like God tells us and as a result we have health issues? And how did they start? We are enticed by our own desire.

The list goes on and on: greed, gossip, pornography, envy, hatred. All of these can ruin our lives.

Consider Bear Grylls, the famous survivalist. If we were in the middle of nowhere and had no idea how to get out, we would do whatever Bear said. We would take our backpack, empty it and only pick up the items Bear told us to—no questions asked.

Doesn't God know life and the human heart better than Bear knows the wilderness? But we keep picking up unhealthy things and putting them in our backpack. And God promises these items will cause some type of loss or death.

I've come to a conclusion that a sin of omission really is a choice and using the "no one is perfect" card is cheap theology.

How content are we with the old nature hanging around our life, causing loss and pain? How desperate are we to have the old nature die? Is it time to address the things that we know should be out of our lives?

When I went to stay at Mayo, Julie and I had been married for 36 years. During that time, for three months, she was with me 24-7. Our friends prayed more for her than me because…well, let's just say that being with me for over 2,000 hours straight may not be the most enjoyable thing for anyone, including Julie. I can be irritable, self-centered and demanding—not in an intimidating way, more like in a five-year-old child kind of way. At one point, I was taking 25 pills a day. That takes a lot of sorting and managing. I told Julie she had to do all of that for me and just give me the pills when I needed them. She had another idea.

"Do it yourself, John," she said. Julie knew I needed to stay mentally engaged in the process. After not talking to Julie for three days (okay, so maybe I was more like a three-year-old than a five-year-old), I realized she was right. Did I tell Julie she was right? Well, if she reads this book, you could say I have.

That little tiff got me to start reflecting on things. Why, I wondered, do I act and think the way that I do? So I started to journal my thoughts. I did not journal daily—only when I felt there was something to say, or there was a thought I was processing. These are some of my journal entries:

March 2

The last five days have been tough. I developed significant sores in my mouth and throat. This made it very difficult to eat. I've been on a liquid diet and even swallowing has been hard. I also shaved my head because my hair was falling out.

That one condition, the hair loss, didn't prevent me from doing anything I wanted. I just shaved my head and moved on. The second condition affected my total being. It affected my sleep, my drinking, my eating, my ability to talk. Everything else was great with me, but this condition dominated my existence.

So far, this experience has caused me to draw a couple of conclusions:

Conclusion 1–I got a small glimpse of what life is like for those that have one condition that dominates their general health, like cerebral palsy or certain forms of autism. There is so much inside the person, but they can't demonstrate or share because the one thing dominates their entire existence.

Conclusion 2–Sometimes I treat sins like these two conditions: 1. My throat was affecting my entire being, therefore I was very motivated in doing what I needed to do to remove this ailment. I did not want to live like this. 2. But losing my hair, I really didn't care. I could live with that. Are there sins in my life today that I tolerate because they aren't affecting my day to day very much? (I think so!)

Lord, help me to seek out all my sins and remove them, just not the debilitating ones.

March 3

Gratitude–one benefit of being afflicted is when the

affliction is removed you have a newfound gratitude.

Today my throat felt much better, and I thanked God for the improvement. I also know that in the future I will at least periodically thank Him for the ability to eat and drink without pain.

So when do I thank God for feet that stabilize me, for legs that move me, for arms and hands that allow me to be independent, for a functional brain, for a house to protect me from the elements, a car that gets me to work? Why does it take having something taken away from you and then being restored to have a grateful heart?

Lord, help me to be grateful for things I take for granted, to realize that there are dozens of gifts, that if taken from me, would completely disrupt my world.

March 7

Rejoice with those who rejoice, weep with those who weep. Something I've been learning about myself. If I feel I have been successful in an area, I find it very easy to root for friends and acquaintances to be very successful, even to be more successful than I may be.

But if I don't have success, or my kids don't have success, it is more of a struggle to root for friends and acquaintances to be successful in that area.

How self-absorbed is that? What does my success or lack thereof, have to do with someone else's journey?

What is the sin I struggle with? Envy, Pride, Resent-ment, Unhealthy competitive spirit?

I think it includes all of them.

Lord, give me a heart that can truly rejoice with those who rejoice and weep with those who weep. Help me overcome envy, pride, resentment, so I can truly want success for all my friends and acquaintances, and their children.

March 15

My health and the positive results to date are based on:

- God's Mercy and Grace on me
- The prayers of people
- My health before the transplant
- My DNA given to me from my parents
- My mental, emotional, spiritual (Faith) condition
- And my doctors and staff at Mayo

They are all important. I believe the last five do play a part but are trumped by the first one.

There have been other people who had better health, better DNA, were stronger mentally, physically and spiritually, yet had terrible results.

There are also people who had more people earnestly praying for them, that did not make it.

Which leaves the final trump card as God's Mercy and Grace.

Why did God heal one and not the other?

Because He loved one more than the other? I strongly doubt that.

Because one had more Faith than the other? I would doubt that too.

Is it because one wanted it more than the others? This answer, too, is no.

Why then? I believe the answer is in the category of God's Mystery. We cannot connect the dots, but we do know that God is always Good. As people of faith, accepting that there are some things that will remain a mystery until we see Him face to face, Mystery is simply part of the Christian Life.

March 18

To claim or not to claim? That is the question!

I have prayed for healing. I have asked for healing. But I have not demanded healing or claimed healing in the name of Jesus.

What is the right way to approach the Throne of God with demands or pleading? Some of the apostles boldly healed people in the name of Jesus. Elijah taunted the priests of Baal before God did a miracle.

If I prayed and demanded that an illness left someone, and it did, would God get the glory or the person who boldly proclaimed it?

Things have been going so well with my medical journey, I know it is God's Mercy and Grace.

Do I claim, "He who began a good work in you will bring it to completion" or "I know the plans I have for you?"

I think those are poster children of Scripture being

misapplied. I think you pray in humility and dependence on His Sovereignty.

Lord, You are the Great Physician, nothing is too hard for You. I pray in the power of Jesus's Name that You would heal me completely. That the new cells would rule my bone marrow 100 percent. Please let that be reflected on this blood test. Please Lord have mercy on me. All Praise and Honor go to You Alone.

March 22

The doctor called me a superstar two days ago. I have been told repeatedly by nurses and providers that they can't believe how well it is going for me.

All the important blood numbers are going in the right direction. My platelets, white blood cells, my neutrophils are now in the normal range and getting close to middle of the normal range instead of the low end of normal.

My hemoglobin hit 10.2 today. The current trend is outstanding. Especially, when I remember the days that it was in the low fives.

I'm in the gym every day now.

I just found out that my CD 33 is 100 percent donor, 0 percent mine, which is great. But my CD 3 which typically lags behind was 40 percent donor and 60 percent mine. The doc said he has no concern at all with these numbers. I then met a fellow patient who had his transplant the same time I did. He is doing well but is still very fatigued. He has a staph infection where he has to go to the clinic twice a day. But his good news was he was at

100 percent donor for CD 33 and 100 percent donor for his CD 3.

Even though the doctor called me a superstar, my blood numbers are doing great, and I feel great, guess what the one thing I'm thinking about continuously?

Why is that guy's CD 3 100 percent and mine is only 40 percent?

The lack of trust in the Father who has been so Gracious to me during this journey is embarrassing. The doc says, "No worries," and yet I'm thinking about that number more than all the great numbers. The doc said my CD 3 is somewhat typical and yet I'm a little anxious.

God, forgive me for doubting you. Forgive me for the lack of patience, forgive me for my envy and jealousy. *"Have no anxiety about anything. But in everything with prayer and supplication, with thanksgiving, let your requests be made known to God. And the Peace of God that passes all under-standing will keep your hearts and minds in Christ Jesus."*[4]

I've known that passage by memory forever, yet am I applying it? It does me little good to memorize hundreds of passages in Scripture if I don't make them my own. I need to be quiet in the presence of God and trust in Him that He will finish this work He is doing in my body.

Focus on all of the great things going on in my body. Be thankful, be grateful, be humbled by His Goodness and Trust Him for the unknown.

March 25

Accumulation of wealth.

Should I cap my salary? A better question is should I cap what I live on and give the rest to charities? The average Christian gives under three percent of their income to charities. Only five percent give 10 percent of their income. So when Julie and I give more to charities than all other expenses, it puts us in a unique category. As I sit here, why doesn't it feel good? When I focus on what we give, I can be puffed up. When I focus on what we keep, I feel a little different.

Commitment going forward: focus on what I keep.

April 1

The doctor doesn't want me to go home this weekend, but he knows I am. I really think he isn't that opposed to it, but it is that one in 10,000 chance that something goes terribly wrong and I need immediate attention. I still don't know if Dr. Hassan is a Muslim or Christian, but he did say I have been blessed. (P.S.: Found out later he is a Muslim.)

I've still been working out at the gym 19 of 21 days. My cardio is better and my body is getting toned. I hope I can keep that up when I get home. This weekend will be a good test. I want to exercise at least two of the four days. (P.S.: I didn't!)

April 2

Read devotion from the book *Abide in Christ* by Andrew Murray. He made a great point. I know how imperfect my love is, but I love my son and daughters a lot. So it is not a stretch to understand the perfect love the Father has for His Son, Jesus. He loved the Son beyond measure.

John 15:9 says, *"As the Father has Loved Me, so have I Loved you, abide in My Love."*[5] So we are told by Jesus that Jesus loves us, just as the Father loved Him. Jesus has the perfect Love for those who follow Him. But for us to really live in that Love, we have to give up all to Him, so He can work all in us.

Just as Jesus fully obeyed the Father in all things and even went to the Cross, it was the perfect love of the Father, and the Son. Jesus was all in, and in every way.

We need to be all in and give Jesus all we have that we may experience and live in this Love of which the world has very little understanding. Like the Cross, it is a free gift, but it costs you all of your illusions of power, control, and self-sufficiency. Only when we give up all these illusions can we really see the beauty of our Savior.

This love gives all, but also asks for all. He freely gives, but He does not freely take. He has left that up to us.

Will we give all?

April 4

The Father's Representative is Jesus Christ (and it was a perfect representation). Jesus Christ's representation is us (2 Corinthians 5: 18-20 calls us His Ambassadors). How are we doing? How am I doing?

April 10

The Fear of the Lord is the beginning of Wisdom.[6]
Let that always be on my heart.

When I get rattled, I still can see what is in me. But I have actually seen some growth. Getting my meds this month was a disaster. I was told one thing by one person and another person would tell me the exact opposite.

For example, I opened an email, and Anthem told me that the med got re-routed to MN and gave me the routing number to prove it. As I'm reading this email, I get a call from Express Scripts and they tell me it has been shipped and gave me the exact same routing number, but says it is going to my Illinois address and that is where it ended up going.

I know I should have started this process weeks ago and I would not have been up against the wall. So I remained pretty calm and told the people that there was plenty of mud on my shoes.

Now if I can respond this way when someone in the family messes up. God forbid that I've messed up before with the family. Why is it we struggle with showing grace to our children and our spouses?

I guess Jesus's statement "Let he who is without sin cast the first stone" has broader applications than I thought. Good words to remember when I feel myself getting mad.

April 20

One day before Easter. I've been reading a book on the Syrian Civil War called *No Turning Back*. There is a lot of hate in this book. Some of my thoughts:

The most destructive form of cancer ever known to man is "hatred."

Hatred can be or is addictive and progressive. It starts out small. I hate this person. As you feed on this hatred, you start to hate people who like or are loyal to the one you hate. Then it continues to people that you think like him. So you now hate an entire group of people. (Right now there are millions of people in America that actually hate you if you dared to vote or support or even prayed for a sitting president. And it was the same for the president before him and will be the same for the president after him.)

Then you start to hate all people who don't think like you. And then you hate even those that generally think the way you think, but not specifically. (Al Qaeda and ISIS are both radicalized, but they can't agree on how extreme they should be so they kill each other.)

The brutality is incredible. They kill people in the group they once played with. They kill previous friends because they don't embrace the right religion. They kill people in their religion because they don't believe in killing people because they have a different faith.

And once it is that easy to kill, you kill your own friends because of the silliest of arguments.

HATE IS SCARY—KEEP LOVE IN YOUR HEARTS.

May 1

This is the last night as a resident of Rochester, MN.

So what are the 13 lessons I've learned to date?

1. Your caregiver must be your advocate. There is only one who walked on water and he/she doesn't live in Rochester. You need to be engaged in your care. I declined blood transfusions three or four times. And it was a good decision. I know my body and how I feel and what I can handle.

2. Be as healthy as you can get before the journey and put on a few extra pounds if you want because you will lose a fair amount of weight.

3. Try not to use a wheelchair.

4. Have a positive mental attitude. Avoid negative self-fulfilling prophecies.

5. Care for your emotional state as well as your physical.

6. Seek to grow spiritually and be open to what God wants to tell you.

7. Take care of yourself, but minister to others. Life is not about you.

8. As people pray for you, reciprocate and ask for their prayer requests and then pray with your care giver and follow up on the request to see how things are going for them.

9. Don't get too high when you hear news you like and don't get too low when you hear news you don't like. You are going to have both so just accept that as part of the journey.

10. Invest in people who are caring for you and others

going through the same thing. Try to keep your eyes on other people not yourself.

11. Be okay that God is the Sovereign One. Be at peace that this is not our home. Our home is in Heaven. Be okay with the thought of dying, it will remove all fear.

12. Exercise as much as you can.

13. **Never be a contestant on** *Jeopardy!*

THE MOST BAFFLING OF ALL

"John, I have to be honest. Your success... baffles me!"—A good friend

I've shared how my forum group has been good for me in my development as a person. One of the things they do well is not let me get puffed up. During one meeting, we were talking about our businesses and my business. MH Equipment was doing well that month—actually MH had been doing pretty well for quite some time. We were growing organically and through acquisitions. We were making significantly more money than any other business in the group. You would think with this track record, I would be afforded a certain level of respect and possibly reverence.

Nope.

One of my friends said, "John, I don't want you to take this the wrong way, but your success...baffles me!"

My first thought was *I need new friends*. But then a

second thought sprang to mind: *'Baffling' is the perfect way to reflect on any success afforded to me.*

The definition of baffle is "impossible to understand; perplexing." I have not reached business success like millions of others, but any success I have had is a little perplexing. Buying a broken-down company on the verge of bankruptcy in 1994, in an industry I had no aptitude for, with no experience even running a company let alone owning one…yes, it's safe to say that whatever success we have had is surprising.

Even baffling.

Throughout this book I've attempted to share some of my life experiences, my approach to business and my heart. I truly hope that you picked up a few things that will be useful in your journey; maybe there were a few words that inspired you.

I have shared how faith has influenced me. I've shared how I have fallen short. How I have wounded those I love. How I have been in the desert, and lost in what I'm doing.

There is one word that keeps me wanting to do the next right thing, even after I have blown it. And it is possibly the most baffling word of all.

The word is Grace.

Before I define Grace, let me define another word that is precious to me. Mercy! Mercy is defined as "not receiving a bad outcome that could be placed upon you." Let's say you stole a pair of shoes from a store and got caught. If the owner of the store decided not to call the police and instead let you go, that would be an example of mercy.

But Grace is different. Grace is "receiving something good instead of the bad you deserve." For example, if the store owner not only didn't call the police but actually gave you the shoes you stole, that would be Grace.

Grace is not simply getting something that you didn't work to obtain; it's receiving something that you couldn't have gotten any other way. Think of a family that has a young child who needs a lifesaving operation but does not have the money nor the means to get the money to have the operation. Let's say someone, or a group of people, stepped up and paid for the surgery. That family does not lose their self-respect or dignity, but every day for the rest of their life, they will wake up grateful to the people who provided the funds to keep their child alive.

The most baffling example of Grace in the history of man is this guy called Jesus. He comes down from His throne in Heaven, lowers Himself to become a man, lives a perfect life and the world kills Him. That world includes me...and you. As Jesus was dying on the Cross, He took upon Himself the sins (and the penalty of those sins) of the very people that nailed Him to the Cross. He forgave them. That is incredible Mercy. But then He went one step further: He gave His Righteousness to those who believe. He gave us the right standing with God the Father which gives us eternal life. That is baffling Grace!

This is the Grace I embraced years ago. Billions of people have asked over the history of the world, "How do I get to Heaven?" In the New Testament, there was only one person that Jesus guaranteed would have eternal life.

Do you remember? Let's see what Luke wrote when Jesus was crucified between two thieves:

> *One of the criminals who were hanged railed at him, saying, "Are you not the Christ? Save yourself and us!" But the other rebuked him, saying, "Do you not fear God, since you are under the same sentence of condemnation? And we indeed justly; for we are receiving the due reward of our deeds; but this man has done nothing wrong." And he said, "Jesus, remember me when you come into your kingdom." And he said to him, "Truly, I say to you, today you will be with me in Paradise."*[1]

That guy was guaranteed Heaven. We don't even know his name. Yet whatever he believed, Jesus liked it. In a matter of a few words it is revealed how people get to Heaven. I call it "The Gospel of the Sinner on the Cross." He knew that he had a sin issue and he deserved to die because of it. He knew the guy in the middle, Jesus, was innocent and had the answer, that He was the prophesied Christ. He asked Jesus to remember Him. So that is the Gospel—the good news! The bad news: we have to acknowledge we can't make it to Heaven on our own. The good news: Jesus provides a way through the Cross, and our job in this drama is simply receive it!

Being a leader of a company is tough, especially when you are open about your faith. For me, the daily question is: *Do I live the day focusing on me, or do I live the day focusing on being the best version of John Wieland that God desires for me?* Sometimes I do an okay job pursuing how God wants me to serve Him; others, sometimes not so much. I think one of the reasons I fell in love with Jesus is because of what the writer of Hebrews says: *"We have a high priest that understands and sympathizes with our weaknesses."*[2] This means that when we stumble and fall, when we lack faith or are simply lost, Jesus is not in Heaven saying, "John, I'm sick and tired of you. I'm done with you." He is for us, not against us. He knows I am broken. He knows I will never be perfect. He knows I will never be worthy of Heaven on my own merits. He knows that about me and He knows that about you. But out of His Love for the broken, He made a way for eternity with Him in Heaven. The Cross.

THE MOST BAFFLING GRACE OF ALL—JESUS

NOTES

3. Prepare the Child for the Road, Not the Road for Your Child

1. Luke 15: 11-32

10. My Very Own Arch Nemesis

1. Luke 6: 42

15. Count the Cost?

1. Luke 14: 28-32

22. Lasting Contentment

1. Romans 8: 15
2. Mark 10: 13-15
3. Acts 13: 22
4. Psalms 17: 8
5. Psalms 51: 2-4, 10-12

24. Lessons Learned from a Bone Marrow Transplant

1. Isaiah 55: 6-8
2. Galatians 5: 16-17
3. James 1: 14-15
4. Philippians 4: 6-7

5. John 15: 9
6. Proverbs 1: 7

The Most Baffling of All

1. Luke 23: 39-43
2. Hebrews 4: 15

ACKNOWLEDGMENTS

The stories I shared include the lives of other people and all of them graciously supported me in telling my story.

Thank you as well to...

Tom Spurgeon for giving me an interest in his company that provided the seed money for me to purchase MH Equipment.

The Hyster company for taking a chance on a 35-year-old know-nothing entrepreneur wannabe and supporting me as their dealer.

Jim Boerckel for his incredible giftedness in creating the illustrations to enhance the stories shared in our book.

Anna David, Kaitlin Anthony, Jennifer Champion and the rest of the team at Launch Pad. The entire team was professional and knowledgeable and helped create a read-worthy book. I could not be happier with them.

Amy, Annie and Becky for spending hours and hours reviewing the manuscript and making great recommendations!

My siblings Felicia, Dick and Mel, who graciously allowed me to poke fun at my upbringing, which unfortunately included them.

My forum group—Chuck, Nate, Andy, Bill, Mike, Terry and Win—who encouraged me to go for it and have always challenged me when I reflect behavior that doesn't align with who I want to be.

Mom and Dad for teaching me so much about life, not by your words but by your actions.

Jessica, Jennifer, Jamie and Josiah for giving me insight on this book and for letting me use their stories.

Julie for being the ultimate Proverb 31 woman: "A woman who fears the Lord is to be praised."

Jesus, whose Mercies are new every morning.

ABOUT THE AUTHOR

John Wieland purchased a small, virtually bankrupt company in 1994. Under his leadership, MH Equipment has gone from having three branches and 50 employees to having over 900 employees and over 30 branches. Wieland is also the president of the His First Foundation, a nonprofit that receives 10 percent of MH's profits. He teaches college graduates how to handle money responsibly, is a speaker and will guest preach from time to time. He and his wife Julie have four children: Jessica, Jennifer, Jamie and Josiah. Contact him at uncommonthreadsbook@gmail.com using the subject line of *Uncommon Threads*.